ROMANS IN MORAY
THE EVIDENCE

ROMANS IN MORAY
THE EVIDENCE

IAN KEILLAR

First published in 2005
by Moray New Horizons
1 Linksfield Court,
Elgin, Moray IV30 5JB

Printed by MMS Almac Ltd.

ISBN 0-9551137-0-9

Layout and page make-up by Helen Williamson
Typeset in Baskerville MT 11/15 pt
Cover by Selena Art Design

The author and publishers wish to acknowledge the support of The
Moray Council.

Moray New Horizons has been established to assist into print books
with new insights about Moray, its heritage and its future.

This book is dedicated to the memory of the late
Professor G. D. Barri Jones of Manchester University,
who died on 16th July 1999

Foreword

It has given me very great pleasure to accept the invitation to write a brief introduction to Ian Keillar's book. I am not a Romanist but my interest in Scottish place names has inevitably led me to being confronted by their function during the Roman period; I am not an expert on Moray either but my pursuit of the significance of place names in the prehistoric landscape of the Scottish north-east has just as inevitably brought me into contact with the author of this book, and it has been a great privilege to observe at close hand his persistent, often frustrating and frustrated, but in the end gratifyingly fruitful, investigations into the presence and role of the Romans in Moray. Historically, Moray is, of course, as the author makes clear, a much larger entity than the areas so designated by current or recent administrative divisions, and this fact is appropriately reflected in the regional coverage of this study.

It must have given the author great satisfaction to be able to add to the title of the book - *Romans in Moray* - the phrase *The Evidence,* thus once and for all removing the subject matter from the realms of speculation and scholarly bickering. As the members of the Moray Field Club and others interested in the archaeology of the region well know, the pursuit of the Romans in Moray has for several decades now been locally almost synonymous with the name Ian Keillar, and his cooperation with the team of archaeologists around the late Barri Jones has been particularly successful in that respect, demonstrating how effective the dovetailing work of the academic professionals and the knowledgeable local researcher can be, especially if the latter has the original vision. There can be hardly anything more persuasive regarding this claim than the theme of the conference in conjunction with which this book is launched – the subsequent Roman finds at Birnie, particularly the spectacular coin hoards in their tangible, datable and socially significant confirmation of that vision and of the combined efforts to give it actuality. Previous publications by the author had, of course, already provided an intimation of his preoccupation: his 1986 examination of 'In Fines Borestorum' in *Popular Archaeology;* his 1993 account with Barri Jones and Keith Maude, of 'The Moray Aerial Survey:

discovering the prehistoric and protohistoric landscape' in the Scottish Society for Northern Studies volume on *Moray: Province and People;* his 1999 article on 'The Romans in Moray' in the *Moray Field Club Bulletin* 27; and his 2002 paper, with G. D. B. Jones, on 'The Archaeological Landscapes of Moray' in *Northern Scotland* 22.

It is for this reason not surprising, and must have been almost unavoidable, that there are several autobiographical touches, both overt and covert, in this book but, instead of allowing such references to become dominant or even overwhelming, Keillar has deftly incorporated them in what is more than anything else a readers' presentation, whether these are professionals, academics, or the people of Moray with an interest in their heritage of the Roman kind. What is therefore particularly noteworthy in this two-pronged, or multi-pronged tactic is the way in which the wide sweep of its approach ('Moray: the Land and the Strategy', 'Ancient Historians', 'Modern Writers') tapers via a well-directed focus on the Imperial Roman Army and Navy into informative descriptive detail of Roman sites in Moray – possible, probable and positive – and, how could it be otherwise, finally an almost celebratory highlighting of Birnie and its hoards, minted in the last decade of the second century AD. Many of the details show the skilled touches of the Chartered Engineer who came to Moray in 1964 to work for the North of Scotland Hydro-Electric Board, from a critical assessment of Ptolemy's identification and positioning of *Tuesis* to the size of a Roman legion and its precise spatial requirements in a camp.

Thus this book informs, assesses, criticises, confirms, persuades and, what is most important, convinces, and becomes an octogenarian's testimony to a full life's strivings and the achievements of a group of people, of which the author is an essential member. In its overview as well as its minutiae, it is soundly opinioned but never opinionated, and its publication makes a welcome contribution to the literature on both Moray and the Romans in Scotland.

W. F. H. Nicolaisen
University of Aberdeen

Romans in Moray

Foreword

Preface

Figures

Plates

Preface

It is the author's privilege, nay, duty, to write a preface in which the author thanks all those to whom he is indebted, but to whom he does not intend to send a free copy of his book. Then the author conventionally thanks the spouse or bidie-in who has endured, or perhaps even enjoyed, the long hours of separation which the writing of any book entails.

I came to Moray in 1964 as a Chartered Engineer with the North of Scotland Hydro-Electric Board. The area I worked in extended from Unst in the north of Shetland to Ballachulish in the south and from Barve in the Western Isles to beyond Banff in Buchan. As I travelled over the area I gradually appreciated that not all the stories I heard of Roman roads and camps were the product of too much imagination and locally distilled whisky. I was not alone in my belief. For ten years, starting in the early nineteen seventies, I was much encouraged by the annual excursion up north of General Jim Scott-Elliot, one time President of the Society of Antiquaries of Scotland, and a talented dowser. From him I learnt the art of reading the landscape and the importance of secure supply lines.

However, it was obvious that plodding about on the ground, even with the assistance of a dowser, was not the best way to discover sites; Roman or otherwise. After Jim retired from his Roman field activities I took to the air and in 1983 flew over Tarbat, Portmahomack and Birnie, noting auspicious sites for future revisiting. At about this time Professor G. D. Barri Jones of Manchester University heard about my activities and, encouraged by his interest, I and two others established the Moray Aerial Archaeology Group with a combined initial investment of £1,000. The aims and objects of the Group were the furtherance of the study of the geology, landscape, archaeology and history of the Moray Firth area, with particular reference to the use of aerial reconnaissance and photography. It was soon obvious that Barri was much better at aerial reconnaissance than I was and amongst his discoveries, funded by the

Group, were the sites at Portmahomack and Birnie. Both sites have been subject to extensive excavation over the last few years. For over fifteen years we worked together, until, in 1999, a sudden heart attack, while walking in his beloved Welsh mountains, took Barri away on the very eve of an extensive scheme of aerial photography which we had planned for that summer.

Barri's photographic archive was left in some disorder and there are several interesting photographs which have not yet been provenanced. However, most of his photographs associated with Scotland have now been archived with the RCAHMS, together with the few where I held the copyright. My earlier files concerning the Romans have also been archived by the Royal Commission and the latest will join them, subsequent to the publication of this book.

To thank all those who have contributed to my search for the Romans would take up the remainder of this book. There is a short dedication in Bodø cathedral which is more eloquent than a superfluity of words: 'None named and none forgotten'. Conventionally, I thank my wife and family, who, when younger, were 'encouraged' to accompany their father on wanderings over the bogs and braes. David Milne for his hard work on the dour Banff subsoil and his ability to recognise periglacial frost shattering, and Sinclair Ross for his informed scepticism. Kenny Williamson for his enthusiasm and the pictures of the first coin hoard being uncovered. Stan Wolfson's classical knowledge and gentle humour have been indispensable. Above all, I thank my friend and critic, W. Ashley Bartlam for his help, tolerance and corrective influences upon me.

Ian Keillar
2005

CHAPTER I
Moray - The Land and the Strategy

The boundary of the present local authority of Moray is but a pale shadow of the once proud diocese of Moray which stretched from the Spey to the Western ocean and south to the marches of Atholl. The earldom of Moray was also extensive and so this description of Roman, and possible Roman, sites within Moray is not constrained by the limits of modern bureaucracy but extends beyond these bounds, which have an elasticity of meaning of which the Red Queen in *Alice Through the Looking Glass* could only approve *[Figure 1]*.

Moray, although geographically within the Highland Line, comprises the low-lying littoral on the south side of the Moray Firth and, sheltered by the mountains from the worst of the weather, has a remarkably mild climate for an area which shares the same general latitude with the cities of Moscow and Churchill, in which latter town polar bears have been known to raid the dustbins. In addition to the North Atlantic Drift, which warms up the whole of Britain as well as North-West Europe, Moray is especially favoured by the föhn effect, whereby the prevailing south-west wind deposits most of its moisture on the hills around Fort William and, once over the high ground, the dryer air is then compressed and warmed as it falls down into Moray.

To early peoples, well exposed to the vagaries of the weather, the climatic advantage of Moray would not have gone unnoticed. The Clava Cairns and the number of other cairns, standing stones etc., now, alas, many destroyed, pay mute testimony to the extent that Moray was once, and still is, considered a desirable place to live. Medieval monks had an eye for a good site, and not only was the Diocese of Moray established initially near Elgin and eventually within Elgin, but there were

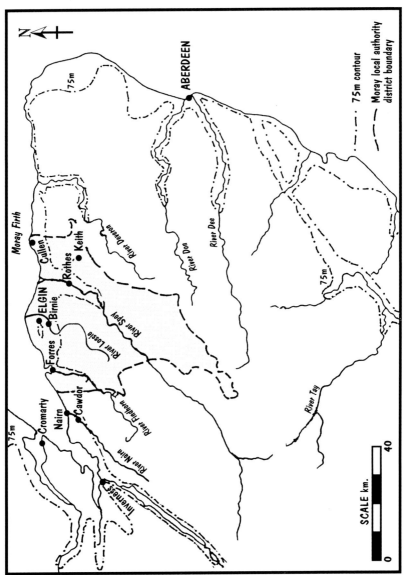

Figure 1: Moray: Modern Boundaries

Benedictines at Urquhart, Cistercians at Kinloss and Valliscaullians at Pluscarden as well as Black and Grey Friars within Elgin. As Sir Robert Gordon of Straloch (1580-1661) wrote:

> *In salubrity of climate, Moray is not inferior to any, and in richness and fertility of soil, it much exceeds our other northern provinces. The air is so temperate, that when all around is bound up in the rigour of winter, there are neither lasting snows nor such frosts as damage fruits or trees; proving the truth of the boast of the natives, that they have forty days more of fine weather in every year than the neighbouring districts.... Corn, the earth pours forth in wonderful and never failing abundance. Fruits of all sorts, herbs, flowers, pulse, are in the greatest plenty, and all early.... The earth is almost always open, the sea navigable, and the roads never stopped.*

The rainfall is generally low, circa 70cm per annum, but occasionally, if a deep depression drifts in from the north-east then the rivers can rise with remarkable speed and cause extensive flooding with consequent damage. The most famous widespread flood occurred in 1829 and was written about by Sir Thomas Dick Lauder (1873), but there were more recent floods in July 1997 and November 2002 and, although geographically restricted, yet were devastating in their impact. The area is drained by six rivers which rise in the south-west and, following ancient water courses, discharge into the Moray Firth. Many of these rivers have developed wide flood plains which were extensively deployed during the last war as airfields and, with their well-drained level gravel surfaces, were also attractive to earlier settlers *[Figure 2]*.

The furthest west, and the shortest, of these rivers is the Ness which flows from the loch of the same name and passes through the town of Inverness to the sea. A few miles east is the river Nairn which, like the Ness, also flows through the similarly named town. Until the last three hundred years or so, Nairn was known as Invernairn and in the days of James VI was the boundary between the Highlands and the Lowlands.

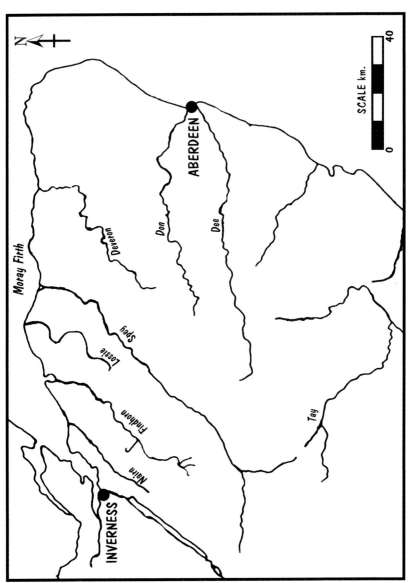

Figure 2: Moray: Drainage Pattern

To the west the people spoke Gaelic but on the east side of the river it was Scots. Further east again is the Findhorn, draining an extensive catchment area and flowing through generally unrewarding ground. Subject to flash floods, it was once a fine salmon river and supplied the markets of London with salted fish as well as keeping lawyers busy as the monks of Kinloss and the bailies of Forres disputed their respective fishing rights (Cuthbert 1998:48-49).

Flowing through Elgin is the tiddler of the rivers, the Lossie. A thousand years or so ago the Lossie may well have flowed west into a estuary near the Findhorn, but in one of its more splenetic spates the Lossie turned sharply east at Aldroughty and ever since has flowed through the City and Royal Burgh of Elgin. By circa 1190 (Barrow 1971:356), there was a mill on the Lossie and since then the river has served the community and occasionally terrorised it.

Next comes the Spey. This brawling tumbling river, fed with winter snows and summer storms, can still frighten the neighbourhood. It was bridged in the Middle Ages (REM 1837:120), but it was not until the early years of the 19th century that there was a road crossing over it at Fochabers. The bridge lasted but a few years when the Muckle Spate of 1829 carried part of the structure and a capering youth down to the mighty sea (Lauder 1873:152-3). Telford's elegant bridge at Craigellachie survived only because the locals, in Telford's absence, had been able to persuade his assistant and the contractor to build the bridge some 12ft higher than intended. The Spey has been declared a navigable river, but only canoes and rafts are capable of safely floating down the river from Rothiemurchus to the sea. Outwith the confines of modern Moray, and not having the benefits of the milder Moray climate, is the Deveron; a somewhat sluggish river but with a valley conducive to settlement, both ancient and modern.

It is difficult to visualise Moray as it was even two hundred years ago. Then there were many more lochs and mosses and sometimes their names continue to this day *[Figure 3]*. Lochinver is now the name

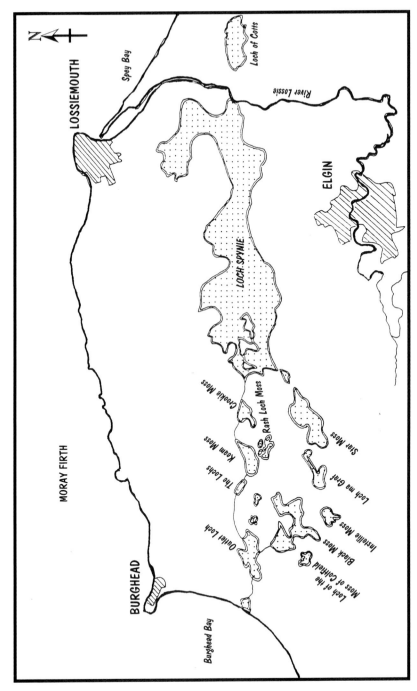

Figure 3: The Lochs and Mosses in the Laich of Moray, circa 1749, from Ross (1992)

of a croft, while Loch of Cotts is still used to describe a piece of low land which is liable to flooding during the winter. Gilston Loch, in living memory, was filled with chilly water as soldiers under training swam across it in battle gear with rifle and steel helmet balanced precariously on the top of their packs. The loch was subsequently filled in using demolished concrete from the surplus-to-requirement runways at the adjacent airfield. Further back in time there was open water between Findhorn and Lossiemouth. Burghead sat on a peninsula, allegedly turned into an island by a series of ditches dug across its neck. Lossiemouth was only a twinkle in the eyes of some future Elgin Town Councillors while the sea swished past unimpeded from south of Burghead to where Lossiemouth now stands.

Earlier still, circa 12,000BC, the Ice Age was coming to an end and the glaciers retreated to the hills of the north-west, their raging melt waters dumping piles of sand here and heaps of gravel there. Drumlins and eskers abound, and on the tops of these desirable and well drained sites, the Neolithic and Bronze Age peoples built their farms. Populations came and went. Languages developed and died. The climate changed. Far-distant volcanoes brought inexplicably bad harvests and the singular slumping of sediment in the North Sea sent a tidal wave of ferocious proportions sweeping through any coastal settlements. By about 700BC, bronze tools had given way to iron and the Celtic speaking people lived in small communities in thatch roofed round houses, grinding their grain in trough querns and generally living at peace with their neighbours.

In far away Rome, a tiny city state was tired of being bullied and decided to teach its neighbours a lesson. Over the next few hundred years that city state subdued not only its near neighbours but more distant and powerful nations, such as Carthage and Egypt, while it even disputed territory with the powerful Persians (Gilliver 2001:52). Gaul, despite the best efforts of Asterix, was brought to heel by Julius Caesar (1972) while across the Rhine the Germans put up a stiff resistance to the Romans (la Baume 1975:10-11). North of Gaul and just across a narrow stretch of water lay the island of Britain, a rich source of rumours, lead, tin, pearls, corn, slaves and saboteurs. There were no doubt complex reasons for bringing it into the ambit of the Roman sphere of influence. It would tidy up the map, release manpower otherwise spent in guarding the coast of Gaul etc. etc. The generals had their reasons and the traders and con merchants no doubt had theirs. A *causus belli* is usually complex, seldom simple and never, ever, honest.

Julius Caesar invaded Britain in 55BC and spent some two months in southern England until storms dispersed his fleet and he had to withdraw. In 54BC, with a much larger force, comprising some 800 ships, he reinvaded, but again storms damaged the fleet and after negotiations with the local tribesmen, Caesar quietly returned to Gaul. In the subsequent years, trade between Britain and Gaul increased. The British rulers continued their internal bickering, with the occasional disgruntled politician seeking refuge in Rome, while, in the reverse direction, continental rulers who had fallen foul of their Roman masters, took refuge in Britain. From the Roman point of view the situation in southern Britain was not stable and the emperor Claudius took the decision to invade the island (Frere 1987:16-26).

Early in AD43 an army of 40,000 men, comprising four legions and associated auxiliary troops and cavalry was assembled at Boulogne under the command of Aulus Plautius. His first difficulty was that the navy mutinied as they did not wish to sail into the unknown, well beyond the proper boundaries of the world. Claudius despatched a minister from Rome to speak to the recalcitrant sailors and they returned to their duties. The force arrived at Richborough, to the surprise of the locals who thought that the navy was still mutinous (Frere 1987:48-62). Within a few years the Romans were pushing the recalcitrant natives north and west. Collaborators were doing splendidly, as the Romans knew very well the tricks necessary to ensure compliance with the minimum of coercion. Occasionally, as in Jerusalem (Josephus 1959:137-8), and in Britain with the Iceni (Cottrell 1958:132-145), the local Roman administrators became too greedy and extortion was followed by repression and this led to revolt.

In the land of the Iceni, the revolt was led by their queen, Boudicca. The mob she whipped up was murderous, vengeful and sadistic; but it was just a mob, and after burning Colchester and London it met the discipline and cold steel of Suetonius Paulinus with the XIVth Legion, part of the XXth Legion and such auxiliaries and cavalry as he could assemble. In total he had about 10,000 men facing the majority of the able-bodied adults of the Iceni plus associates from adjoining tribes. The mob howled and raged but the legions were fighting, not only for their lives, but to revenge the truly dreadful fates of their pensioned colleagues, wives and children. Discipline triumphed over the mob (Frere 1987:21-3). Boudicca committed suicide and, after a suitable time to reorganise, the Roman army continued with its march west and north into the remainder of Britain.

Anybody attempting to conquer or govern Britain must subdue the northern part of the mainland, now known as Scotland. As Shakespeare puts it rather bluntly in Henry V Act 1 Scene2:

> But there's a saying, very old and true:,
> 'If that you will France win,
> Then with Scotland first begin'
> For once the eagle England being in prey,
> To her unguarded nest the weasel Scot
> Comes sneaking and so sucks her princely eggs,
> Playing the mouse in absence of the cat,
> To tear and havoc more than she can eat.

For centuries, England never felt secure with a usually hostile Scotland to the north. Edward I tried, somewhat too brutally, to bring Scotland to heel, while his effete son, Edward II, also tried and failed miserably at Bannockburn (Nicholson 1974:87-91). Later, Henry VIII tried force, diplomacy and dynastic marriage to subdue his northern neighbour, and while Scotland was considerably distressed it did not succumb. Eventually James VI, king of Scots, went down to London to become James I of England, but even his obvious enthusiasm for an outright union did not catch on with his Scottish subjects. It was to be a hundred years later, when years of bad harvests in Scotland, followed by the Darien disaster and the lure of gold, allowed the English to say 'now we have catched them, we will never let them go.'

But the English, now that they were de facto governors of all mainland Britain, while they fully appreciated the strategic importance of holding Scotland, they perhaps did not immediately realise the significance that to hold Scotland, they must keep a tight grip on Moray. The early kings of Scots well knew the importance of Moray. A rich and fertile land, tucked away behind the mountains, could be, and often was, the source of rebellion and revolt. In the days when information was carried at the speed of a galloping horse, it was essential that incipient trouble could be crushed before it could grow and develop. Early kings, such as Duncan I and Duncan II, both died in Moray, the former in battle against Macbeth, the Mormaer of Moray in AD1040. Accordingly, later kings such as William and Alexander II were ruthless in their extirpation of what they considered treason (Duncan 1975:193-200,528-529). However it was not sufficient to conduct lightning raids into Moray but it was essential to establish a stable government, loyal to a distant king sitting several days' march away. Barrow (1980:61-117) describes the process whereby native nobility 'must in practice have been elbowed to one side or simply replaced.' Foreigners, owing allegiance only to the king, were invited from Normandy, Frisia and the Low Countries, to take up land, establish castles and, above all, ensure that the peasants professed loyalty, through their lord, to the king in far-distant midland Scotland (Davies 1990).

One Englishman who well knew of the significance of Moray was that canny Hammer of the Scots, Edward I. Twice he visited Moray, in 1296 and 1303, and established English garrisons in all the castles within the Royal burghs. Following his first visit, resistance to the English developed in the south under Wallace and under Andrew Moray in the north. As Nicholson (1974:50) ruefully comments, 'No details survive of the campaign that Andrew Moray must have waged in the following five weeks to obtain mastery of the whole region north of Tay.' Without control of Moray it is impossible to control Scotland and after the deaths of Moray and Wallace, Edward I reinstalled English garrisons in Moray. When Robert the Bruce eventually took over as leader of the Scottish freedom fighters, he systematically went about destroying the English strongholds in the north, and it was only after this was accomplished that he felt secure enough to face the decisive battle of Bannockburn. Over three hundred years later, when Montrose was fighting to establish the authority of Charles I over Scotland, he started his campaign at Fort William in February 1645 and later that same year, with victories at Auldearn and Alford, cleared the king's enemies from Moray and Aberdeen, only then did he march south to eventual defeat at Philiphaugh (Donaldson 1965:333-5).

A hundred years after the brilliant Montrose, there arrived in Scotland the unforgettable and hopelessly incompetent Prince Charles Edward Stuart: Bonnie Prince Charlie to his devotees. The Prince bumbled his way south, ignoring the advice of his competent second-in-command, George Murray. After turning back at Derby, the Prince with his exhausted and much depleted Highland army, retreated into the last stronghold available to him, the land of Moray. Neglecting to attack the Hanoverian army as it crossed the Spey, the Prince retired further west with his diminishing army to Culloden Moor, where on the 16th April 1746 the starving Highlanders were mown down by artillery fire until, in desperation, they made a ragged charge on the Redcoat lines. The result was inevitable, but the reputation of the British army was not enhanced by what followed. Murder, rape and theft are charges which can be legitimately laid on Cumberland's army (Prebble 1967:142-158).

In all these seminal activities, either the initial or final military actions for the control of Scotland took place in Moray. Moray was, and continues to be, too important to be ignored in any military activities. During the last war there were nine Air Force bases in greater Moray and two of these are still very much on active service. Control of Moray is essential to the control of Scotland, and this elementary fact is one which those superb military strategists, the Romans, were not likely to ignore.

References

Barrow, G. W. S. *Regesta Regum Scottorum II: The Acts of William I*, Edinburgh. 1971

Barrow, G. W. S. *The Anglo-Norman Era in Scottish History*, Edinburgh. 1980

Baume, P. la *The Romans on the Rhine*, Bonn. 1975

Caesar, J. *The Conquest of Gaul*, Penguin. 1972

Cottrell, L. *The Great Invasion*, London. 1958

Cuthbert, O. D. *A Flame in the Shadows*, Orkney. 1998

Davies, R. R. *Domination and Conquest*, Cambridge. 1990

Donaldson, G. *Scotland - James V to James VII*, Edinburgh. 1965

Duncan, A. A. M. *Scotland - The Making of the Kingdom*, Edinburgh. 1975

Frere, S. *Britannia - A History of Roman Britain*, London. 1987

Josephus, F. *The Jewish Wars*, Penguin. 1959

Lauder, T. D. *The Moray Floods*, 3rd edition, Elgin. 1873

Nicholson, R. *Scotland: The later Middle Ages*, Edinburgh. 1974

Prebble, J. *Culloden*, Penguin. 1967

REM = Cockburn, H. T. ed. *Registrum Episcoptus Moraviensis (Moray Register)*, Edinburgh. 1837

Shakespeare, W. *Henry V, Act 1, Scene 2*

Chapter II
Ancient Sources

The earliest extant map is the Turin papyrus from Egypt, dated to approximately 1,300BC (Posener 1962:112). It was to be almost 1,500 years later before the first practical map of Britain appeared and survived. During this lengthy period of time the ancient Greeks were experimenting with map making, mainly celestial, although Anaximander of Miletus (c.611 - 546BC) is reputed to have produced the first Greek terrestrial map. By the time of Herodotus (c.484 - 425BC) maps were in use by the elite, even though they realised that there was much of the world not represented upon them. Alexander the Great (356-323), a pupil of Aristotle, took secretaries with him on his expeditions to record the geography, soil, flora and fauna of all the countries he conquered (Dilke 1985:29). Unfortunately, none of these reports have survived. Alexander founded the city of Alexandria as a lasting tribute to Greek civilisation. One of his successors, Ptolemy (c.283BC), no relation of the celebrated map maker, founded the great library which continued for almost a thousand years until wantonly destroyed by the Muslim conqueror, Caliph Omar, in AD642. A director of the library, Eratosthenes (c.275 - 194BC) measured the circumference of the earth with astonishing accuracy. His figures, converted from stadia into kilometres, gave a circumference of 40,000 against the actual modern measurement of 45,000km. He is also believed to have produced a map of the known world, including the British Isles with Ireland.

Geographers and maps may well have existed in the three hundred years following Eratosthenes and we do know of one, Marinus of Tyre, whose work the map maker, Claudius Ptolemaeus, now referred to as Ptolemy (c.AD90 - 168), initially praised, then constructively criticised and finally savagely attacked. In this, Ptolemy was in no way different

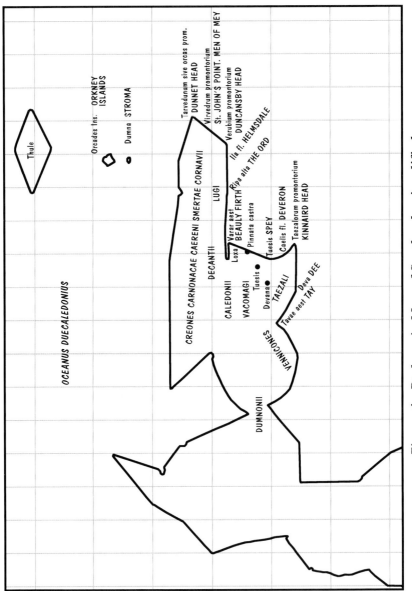

Figure 4: Ptolemy's Map of Scotland - simplified

from too many modern scholars who behave similarly. Ptolemy was a Greek who lived in the Greek city of Alexandria, where he would have had access to the famous library. Amongst the works he studied there must have been the writings of Marinus (c.AD100) which may have supplied some of the raw data from which Ptolemy worked.

Ptolemy produced eight books in which he mapped out the then known world. Book I contains much valuable background information on the meridians and parallels used, while also containing various chapters devoted to explaining the errors and omissions of Marinus. Book II is devoted to North-West Europe including Hibernia, Albion (Britain) and Gaul etc. Book III describes the heartland of Europe, Italy, Dacia, Macedonia etc. Book IV is restricted to Africa, Mauritania, Cyrenaica, Egypt and Ethiopia. Book V is Asia, what we would call Asia Minor, covering Albania, Cyprus, Palestine, Babylonia and Arabia Deserta. Book VI covers the remainder of known Asia, such as Assyria, Persia, Parthia, Scythia and Arabia Felix. Book VII extends to India, both up to and beyond the Ganges, while the final Book VIII explains adaptations and corrections which should be made in the maps. It is obvious that Ptolemy knew much about the geography of the world, but until recently it was widely believed that he saw the world as a series of co-ordinates and that he never produced an actual map. This view has been effectively challenged by J. Fischer SJ in his introduction to Edward L. Stevenson's monumental work on Ptolemy, first published in 1932 (Stevenson 1991:3-15).

Ptolemy's maps are surprisingly accurate, but there is one notable exception and that is the representation of Scotland, which, in relation to England, is turned some 90° to the right *[Figure 4]*. Many attempts have been made to explain this anomaly. An early attempt was made by Colin Maclaurin (1698-1746), the discoverer of the theorem which bears his name and the somewhat unsuccessful designer of the defences of Edinburgh against Prince Charles Edward Stuart. Maclaurin suggested that the Romans entered Scotland from the west and then crossed over to the east, which led them to mistake the breadth for the length, and as they marched from west to east this led them to mistake that the main axis of the country lay this way (Horsley 1733:288-291). Roy (1793:93) believed that the Map of Britain had been originally produced in two parts which had inadvertently been wrongly joined together. Further explanations were put forward by Bradley (1885:103-47), Flinders-Petrie (1917:12-26) and Richmond (1921:288-301) who argued that the error was due to the observation of a lunar eclipse in Scotland producing a longitude that was in conflict with that already established for London. Richmond then used this argument to justify moving *Castra Pinnata* from its proper position on the Moray Firth to Inchtuthil. Tierney (1959:132-148) gives a thorough review of the theories proposed by most of the earlier commentators including the remarkably prescient views of Berger (1903). Tierney concludes that the turning of Scotland was connected with Ptolemy's 'correction' of Marinus's data. Rivet, in Rivet and Smith (1979:103-47) devotes a whole chapter to Ptolemy's *Geography* and besides reviewing the work of previous commentators explains clearly how Ptolemy used the Greek Milesian notation for numbers. The theme of Ptolemy correcting Marinus is taken up again by Jones and Keillar (1996:43-49) but not before Mann (1990:61) cuts through the difficulties like a sword through the Gordian knot by boldly declaring that the Greeks, with little practical experience of the world, decided that life north of 60°, on the Ptolemaic scale, was impossible and, as nobody lived there, Britain could not extend into those regions and the country was thus rotated into liveable regions. This plausible argument ignores the inconvenient fact that the Greeks were not ignorant stay-at-homes, but were, particularly under Alexander, travellers in far-off distant lands. Whatever the reason for the turning of Scotland or Alba, it does not invalidate the spatial relationship between the places allocated latitudes and longitudes by Ptolemy. As Watson (1926:8) points out, 'the outline of the map constructed from the data which Ptolemy supplies is very creditable, and we shall see reason to believe that his names of tribes and places deserve great respect.'

Just as the turning of Scotland has resulted in much speculation, so has the location and identification of the place-names on Ptolemy's map. Horsley (1733:364-378) places *Tuesis* at Nairn and after discussing *Banatia* makes the wise comment: 'but I leave the particular town or spot to be determined by those, who are better acquainted with the Country.' Acting on this admonition, the discussion which follows is limited to that part of the north and east coasts of which the writer has personal knowledge.

Ptolemy properly places *Thule*, Shetland, beyond *Orcades Insulae*, Orkney; while between *Orcades Insulae* and what is now Scotland lies the island of *Dumna*. Rivet & Smith (1979:342) identify it with the Western Isles, but the Western Isles are better identified with *Aebuda Insulae*, now corrupted into the Hebrides. Taking account of the position of *Dumna*, perhaps it should be identified with modern Stroma. *Tarvedunum sive orcas promontorium* must be Dunnet Head with its proximity to Orkney and its characteristic bull-nosed appearance from the sea. Richmond (1921:288-301), Rivet & Smith (1979:469) and Watson (1926:26) – the latter two in particular – bring out the etymological connection between *tarv* and 'bull', and as the site is well described by the name, then *Tarvedunum* can be accepted as a definitely known point in Ptolemy's geography of Britain. *Virvedrum promontorium* is identified by Richmond (1921:288-301), Rivet & Smith (1979:4) and Watson (1926:3) as Duncansby Head, while they unanimously identify *Verubium promontorium* as Noss Head. Jones and Mattingly (1990:map 2.6) equate *Verubium* with Ross Head, a typographical error for Noss Head. Ptolemy locates *Tarvedunum*, *Virvedrum* and *Verubium promontoria* in a straight line, but Dunnet Head, Duncansby Head and Noss Head form a right angle. Noss Head is a low-lying peninsula, not particularly easy to identify from the sea. However, St. John's Point, with the rocks of the Men of Mey off shore and situated in a straight line between Dunnet Head and Duncansby Head, is a maritime hazard which seafarers fear now and would likely to have feared and avoided in the past. As Alexander Lindsay noted in 1540 in his famous rutter (1980:51), 'A half a mile

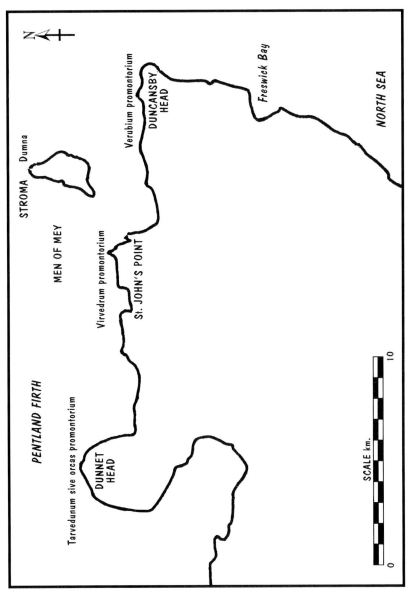

Figure 5: North Coast of Scotland according to Ptolemy

from May Head lyeth dangerous rockis called the Men of May.' The
Men of Mey are a group of offshore rocks round which the restless waters
of the Pentland Firth surge and crash, throwing up showers of spray,
even on a fine day (Rivet & Smith 1979:4). '*Virvedrum*... means something
like very wet (cape) or great wet (cape), presumably with reference to
waves crashing at its foot and sending up spray.' This describes the Men
of Mey and St. John's Point. The *North Coast Pilot* (1975:169), in two
separate paragraphs, gives specific warnings about the Merry Men of
Mey and gives very detailed sailing instructions to mariners on how
best to avoid these rocks. According to Ptolemy, *Tarvedunum*, *Virvedrum*
and *Verubium* are in a straight line, as are Dunnet Head, St. John's Point
and Duncansby Head, so it is reasonable to assume that *Virvedrum
promontorium* is St. John's Point while *Verubium promontorium* is Duncansby
Head *[Figure 5]*.

The next place down the coast is *Ila fluvium*. Watson (1926:47) notes
that the name has survived into the Gaelic as Ilidh, the Helmsdale river.
The Norse renamed Srath Ilidh as the Helmsdale, but the old name
survives; one of the few to be handed down almost intact from the time
of Ptolemy. Richmond (1961:137) baldly states that *Ripa alta* is Tarbat
Ness and Rivet & Smith concur in this. Jones and Mattingly (1990:map
2.6) also show *Ripa alta* as Tarbat Ness but another map (1990:map 1.17)
equates it with the Souters of Cromarty. *Ripa alta* means high bank and
while the Souters are impressive, they are in the plural and are dwarfed
by the high bank of the Ord of Caithness where the cliffs plunge for
almost 200m down into the sea in a scene of grandeur and memorability
well deserving to be called *Ripa alta*.

Before discussing the names along the southern shore of the Moray
Firth, it must be emphasised that Ptolemy was working from notes, or
copies of notes, made by others. He had no idea what the places were
or what their names meant. He was working from confusing data; and
it shows. The information given to Ptolemy was in Greek and, just as in
English, carelessly written letters can lead to misreading. From *Varar*

aest., and along the southern shore of Ptolemy's Moray Firth, only he did not know it by that name, there is *Loxa fl.;* a settlement or fortress site, *Pinnata castra, Tuesis aest., Caelis fl.;* and *Taezalorum promontorium*. Between present day Kinnaird Head, reasonably equated with *Taezalorum promontorium*, and the Beauly Firth, there are five main rivers; the Deveron, Spey, Findhorn, Nairn and Ness but Ptolemy mentions only three. Faced with perhaps too many too similar co-ordinates he simplified matters by dropping the names of two of the rivers. He would, presumably, retain those for which he had particularly good or legible information. Scraps of papyrus or writing tablets with half-melted wax would have been ignored in favour of clearer military despatches.

Sanctified by usage and time, the equation of *Tuesis aest.* with the Spey is universally accepted, though Horsley favoured the Nairn. The Greco/Roman surveyors who provided Ptolemy with his information were meticulous in their differentiation between an estuary and a river, so the *Tuesis* must have had an estuary during the Roman period. An unpublished study by Ross (1990) indicates that for long periods of time there was a substantial estuary on the Spey. An unpublished map by Roy in 1750 also shows a considerable estuary. The name Spey is ancient and either Spey, or something similar to it, was likely to have been current 2,000 years ago. Watson (1926:47) writes: 'Tuesis may well represent the Spey as to position, but not in name.' Nicolaisen (1976:176) states categorically: 'Avon and Spey, names which are of considerable antiquity predating the arrival of any Gaelic... settlers in this part of the country.' Since the Spey is an early pre-Gaelic name, how is it that Ptolemy puts down the name of the river as *Tuesis*? But to add confusion, there is a settlement some slight distance up the river from its mouth which also has the name of *Tuesis*. Whatever the reason for Ptolemy's choice of the name *Tuesis*, it is one which is universally accepted and there seems to be no reason to object to its continuation. In the same way, the identification of *Caelis fl.* with the Deveron is satisfactory with regard to location and need not concern us further. The river Farrar, which flows into the Beauly river, has retained its relationship to *Varar aest.* For as

Watson (1926:19) points out: 'The Varar estuary is undoubtedly the Beauly Firth, for the old name of the Beauly river was Farrar.'

No such certainty applies to *Loxa fl.*, long and uncritically equated with the Lossie, though Watson (1926:48) never subscribed to this view. Richmond (1961:137), with his predilection for moving places around, has no hesitation in transferring *Loxa* from where Ptolemy placed it, west of the Findhorn, to coincide with the Lossie 'to which it is formally equivalent.' Rivet and Smith (1979:448) hedge their bets, while the Ordnance Survey, in its Map of Roman Britain (1956), clearly labels the Lossie as *Loxa fl.* This association of *Loxa* with Lossie, solely on the basis of a perceived similarity in pronunciation, is not tenable. Muddying the waters is the additional perceived similarity between *Loxa* and the Old Norse *Lax*, Modern Swedish *Lax* and the German *Lachs* 'salmon'. Unfortunately for this cosy relationship, first-century fishermen on the river spoke neither Old Norse nor Old German. Any Roman, passing on foot or by boat, would have referred to a salmon as *salmo* while a lost Q-Celtic speaker would have mouthed something about *bradan* (Lhuyd 1963:241). What the local P-Celtic speaking fisherman called the river or the salmon is not known. Modern Welsh takes its name of the fish from the Latin. The correlation between *Loxa* and Lossie is not proven and could well be ignored were it not for the inconvenient Proto-Indo-European word **loksos* meaning salmon, but the splitting of the word into *lok* and eventually *lax* appears to have happened before the Celtic languages broke away from their common ancestry with Greek and Latin. If the meaning of Lossie is connected with salmon, then it is a pathetic salmon river, compared with, say, the Ness or Spey.

However, the subject cannot be left without giving the last word to William Leslie, the irrepressible and eccentric parish minister of Lhanbryde in the early 19th century. 'The Lossie, having now by courtesy the title of river, though but a brook in its ordinary state, being in this parish the drain of 600 square miles, is nevertheless, too inconsiderable to have been heard of in Egypt by Ptolemy, in the beginning of the second century.'

The *Loxa* having been relegated to its more reasonable site at Nairn, this leaves only the position of *Pinnata castra* and the settlement of *Tuesis* to be allocated positions within Moray. According to Ptolemy, *Pinnata Castra*, which is the accepted Latin rendering of πτερωτόυ στρατοπέδου and translates into English as the fort with merlons, is exactly half way between *Varar aest.* and *Tuesis aest.* Placing a rule on a modern map and bisecting the distance between Spey and the Beauly Firth, the putative position of *Pinnata Castra* comes within 1km of Brodie Castle. In September 1940 a Luftwaffe pilot flew over the area and exactly one kilometre from Brodie castle his camera recorded a rectangular crop mark with rounded corners. Is this the *Pinnata Castra* of Ptolemy? *Tuesis polis*, the settlement with the same name as the river, has received surprisingly little attention from the commentators and will be the subject of further discussion later.

About the same time as Marinus was beavering away on his maps, a politician and historian, P. Cornelius Tacitus, more familiarly known to us as Tacitus, was working away on his *Annales*, having recently completed his biography of his father-in-law, Agricola (Ogilvie and Richmond 1967). Tacitus (c.AD55-AD120) married the daughter of the governor of Britain in AD78, and after finishing the biography in AD98 went on to become proconsul of Asia (AD112-AD113). He was a close friend of Pliny, but it is as the author of *De Vita Agricolae* that he is best known in this country. What we know about Agricola has been almost completely influenced by the pen of Tacitus, and while the biography is a most valuable document, it has its limitations and has to be approached with caution.

To a generation, now slipping into the shadows, the word Cassino means a monastery in Italy, dominating the road from the south towards Rome, which in the spring of 1944 was destroyed by the American Air Force and the RAF, and then the ruins were fought over by the youth of America, Germany, Britain and Poland. The monastery has been rebuilt in marble and baroque splendour, but the acres of graves in the plain below are mute witnesses to the folly of war and the true price paid for the reconstruction. In the Middle Ages, it had an extensive, if somewhat neglected, library and about AD1340, ferreting amongst the manuscripts, was a minor early Renaissance and somewhat bawdy poet and raconteur by the name of Boccaccio. He uncovered many of the surviving manuscripts written by Tacitus, including the *Agricola*, the quarry which, mangling the metaphors, has launched a thousand ships and provided fuel for a thousand commentaries.

The works of Tacitus were first printed in 1470 (Burke 1969:149) and during the fifty years from 1600 to 1649, Burke states that sixty-seven editions were published in Europe. By the 18th century, Tacitus, either in Latin or translation, was widespread amongst the educated classes in Britain, and practically every parish minister in Scotland had a copy of Tacitus on his shelf and looked for a Roman station in his glebe. Tacitus, in the *Agricola*, describes the life of his father-in-law and in particular, the seven years when Agricola was governor of Britain, culminating in the epic battle of Mons Graupius. Tacitus tells us where the battle was fought but neglects to give its geographical location or where the Roman fleet over-wintered after the battle, but these omissions do allow for vehement discussion. After Tacitus, a great literary darkness falls upon northern Scotland, periodically and fitfully illuminated by a few sparks from such sources as Cassius Dio, Gildas, Herodian and others.

References

Berger, H. *Geschichte der wissenschaftlichen Erdkunde der Griechen*, Leipzig. 1903

Bradley, H. 'Ptolemy's Geography of the British Isles' in *Archaeologia*. 1885

Burke, P. 'Tacitism' in *Tacitus*, London. 1969

Dilke, O. A. W. *Greek and Roman Maps*, London. 1985

Flinders-Petrie, W. M. 'Ptolemy's Geography of Albion' in *PSAS* Vol. lii. 1917

Horsley, J. *Britannia Romana*, London. 1733

Jones, G. D. B. & Keillar, I. 'Marinus, Ptolemy and the Turning of Scotland' in *Britannia* Vol. xxvii. 1996

Jones, B. & Mattingly, D. *An Atlas of Roman Britain*, Oxford. 1990

Lhuyd, E. *Edward Lhuyd in the Scottish Highlands*, Oxford. 1963

Lindsay, A. *A Rutter of the Scottish Seas*, Maritime Monograph No. 44, Greenwich. 1980

Mann, J. 'The 'Turning' of Scotland' in *PSAS* Vol. cxx. 1990

Nicolaisen, W. F. H. *Scottish Place-Names*, London. 1976

North Coast Pilot, Greenwich. 1975

Ogilvie, R. M. & Richmond, I. *De Vita Agricolae*, Oxford. 1967

Posener, G. et al *A Dictionary of Egyptian Civilization*, London. 1962

Richmond, I. A. 'Ptolemaic Scotland' in *PSAS* Vol. lvi. 1921

Richmond, I. A. *Roman and Native in North Britain*, Edinburgh. 1961

Rivet, A. L. F. & Smith, C. *The Place-Names of Roman Britain*, London. 1979

Ross, S. *Personal Communication*. 1990

Roy, W. *The Military Antiquities of the Romans in North Britain*, London. 1793

Stevenson, E. L. ed. *Claudius Ptolemy - The Geography*, London. 1932, 1991

Tierney, J. J. 'Ptolemy's Map of Scotland' in *Journal of Hellenic Studies* Vol. lxxix. 1959

Watson, W. J. *History of the Celtic Place-Names of Scotland*, Edinburgh. 1926

CHAPTER III
Modern Writers

Of modern writers about the Romans there is a profusion and the consequent selection and presentation of their material gives great scope for bias. And when does one start with the moderns? This decision is completely arbitrary and, in this case, we start with William Camden (1551-1623), who was headmaster of Westminster school and who published the first edition of his *Britannia* in 1586. In 1607 the sixth edition was published and in 1610 this was translated from the Latin into English. In it Camden collected all the then known information about antiquities, particularly Roman material, and his writings were used as a reference source for three hundred years. At the same time as Camden was working in London; in Edinburgh, George Buchanan (1506-1582), one time tutor to James VI whom he treated harshly, even brutally, published his 20-volume *Rerum Scoticarum Historia or History of Scotland*, just before his death. This work is long on legend and even longer on the denigration of Mary Stuart and while, like the curate's egg, it is good in parts, it is not recommended as a primer for the study of the Romans in Scotland. A hundred years after Buchanan, John Aubrey (1626-1697), though trained as a lawyer, spent most of his life collecting information about the antiquities throughout the whole of Britain. Most of it was not published during his lifetime, but a fine edition of his *Monumenta Britannica* was produced in 1982 where he mentions the Antonine Wall and Arthur's O'on but nothing Roman further north. However, he was not entirely ignorant of more remote antiquities, as he notes several of the Aberdeenshire stone circles and the henge at Muir of Ord.

The study of Roman antiquities takes a giant step forward with the publication in 1733 of John Horsley's *Britannia Romana*. John Horsley was born in South Shields in 1684 and graduated at Edinburgh University as MA on 29th April 1701. From 1709 he was the Presbyterian minister at Morpeth where he also ran a private school. He was also a mathematician and he used these skills in his careful examination of the Roman wall which passed within a few metres of his school. Horsley devotes nine pages to detailed drawings of Roman sculptures and altars found in Scotland and the measurements and analysis of his results are well ahead of their time while his 520-page volume, with additional indices, is still worthy of study.

Horsley's volume weighs 4 kilos but this is completely overwhelmed by Roy's *Military Antiquities of the Romans in Britain*, published posthumously in 1793 and measuring 56cm by 38 cm and 5cm deep, weighing in at a massive 7kilos. William Roy was born on 4th May 1726 at Miltonhead near Carluke. Following upon the 1745 campaign and the consequent deficiency in the existing, or rather non-existing maps, plans were set afoot for the mapping of the Highlands. As a civilian helper, Roy had shown great promise and circa 1750 he was commissioned as a lieutenant and eventually reached the rank of Major-General. He mapped practically the whole of Scotland and, in his *Military Antiquities*, not only drew plans of all the then known Roman camps but also mapped those sites which he himself had discovered. His plan and elevation of Burghead is especially valuable as it shows how the headland looked before it was effectively bisected to make the existing harbour. Although his *Military Antiquities* was published in 1793, the work on which it is based took place many years earlier, while Roy's map of Scotland was surveyed no later than 1755, so his book and map illustrate the state of knowledge of the Romans in Britain in the middle of the 18th century. Much of Roy's work is still of value today. His calculations on the number of tents that can be accommodated in a marching camp are as interesting today as when he did his sums two hundred and fifty years ago.

Minor authorities, active during the 18th century, include the Rev. Jameson, whose *Remarks on the Progress of the Roman Army in Scotland During the Sixth Campaign of Agricola* was published in 1786, which, besides containing a good account of the camp at Raedykes, contains an interesting plea for Scotland: 'It gives me pleasure to call the attention of the learned to my neglected country, now become a dispirited province of this British union, and, as cursed with a very bad and inconstant climate, must become the most wretched of all countries on the face of the globe... without resources, without erudition, taste, or morals, to prevent it being crushed under the ruins of an old and wealthy state to which it is now united....'

As the 18th century was drawing to a close there was published one of the greatest records of Scotland ever to appear. This was the *Statistical Account* of every parish in the land, compiled by each kirk minister, the whole orchestrated by Sir John Sinclair of Ulbster (1754-1835). This task took between 1791-1798 and resulted in twenty volumes which were published as and when sufficient parish returns came to hand, so that disparate parishes are to be found side by side. The quality, too, of the returns varies from the perfunctory to the verbose, but it is still a most valuable reference.

George Chalmers (1742-1825) was born in Fochabers, so as a young boy he saw the bedraggled army of Prince Charles pass by on its way to defeat at Culloden, followed by the disciplined red coats of the Duke of Cumberland, otherwise known as Butcher Billy. As a future historian, George Chalmers was witnessing history. After education at Fochabers and King's College, Aberdeen, George moved to Edinburgh and in 1763 emigrated to Baltimore, but returned to Britain on the outbreak of the American War of Independence. He entered politics but his love was historical research and, amongst his many writings, his greatest achievement was the publication of *Caledonia,* an encyclopaedia of Scottish history. Volume I was published in 1807, volume II in 1810 and volume III in 1824. All his research he carried out by himself and while actively involved in his historical work he was also Chief Clerk of the Privy Council and Colonial agent for the Bahama Islands. Near

Fochabers, at Bellie, is a site first noted in Macfarlane's *Geographical Collections* as a Roman camp in 1726 and this was investigated by Chalmers, who, quoting 'an intelligent Colonel Imrie' gives its dimensions as 888ft by 333ft.

Following Chalmers comes a torrent of information, some in the *New Statistical Account*, which appeared in the late eighteen-thirties and early forties and which, unlike its predecessor, was published, county by county. At the same time as the *NSA* was appearing, Robert Stuart in 1845 published his *Caledonia Romana*, the first book devoted entirely to the 'Roman occupation of North Britain'. Stuart is the first to propose that Mons Graupius should be looked for north of the Grampians and he places the battle just south of Banff (Stuart 1845). During the remainder of the century, articles on the Romans appeared in the *Proceedings of the Society of Antiquaries of Scotland (PSAS)* while in 1883 Müller started to publish in Paris the *Ptolemaei Geographiae*, a task not completed until 1901.

The new century brought new writings and new journals devoted to Roman affairs. *The Journal for Roman Studies* started in 1910 and an early issue carried an article by George Macdonald (1919) on 'The Agricolan Occupation of North Britain' where the author advanced the idea that Mons Graupius, and therefore Roman armies, had been further north than previously considered. Pryce and Birley (1938) consider the fate of Agricola's northern conquests and agree that the withdrawal was perhaps not as precipitate as some other authorities would suggest. After the second war, the redoubtable J. K. St. Joseph (1951) took to the air and over fifty years ago he had pushed the Roman presence as far as Auchinhove near Keith, where it has remained for over half a century.

By 1970 there were so many papers on Roman Britain being written that the Society for the Promotion of Roman Studies decided to issue an annual journal devoted entirely to the subject and so was born *Britannia* which has grown and flourished, so that the most recent issue runs to 419 pages. Concurrent with the popularity of *Britannia* there has been a flood of books on all aspects of Roman life, particularly military, and analysis of Agricola and his activities, but few authors have dared to suggest that the Romans crossed the Spey and advanced into Moray. The books which follow have all some relevance to the possibility of the Romans in Moray, but to discuss each in detail would result in duplication, when examining the various sites. Therefore each mentioned book, at this stage, is subjected only to superficial comment.

The premier single volume, covering all aspects of the Roman presence in Britain, is by Frere (1987), and this too is called *Britannia*. Although only a small part of the volume can be allocated to Scotland yet he gives space to argue the case for Bennachie as the site of Mons Graupius and allows himself the latitude to place a question mark to the west of the Spey just beyond Bellie. Was he indicating that he thought there might be Roman sites west of the Spey? Somebody who did believe that the Romans marched west of the Spey was O. G. S. Crawford (1949) whose book *Topography of Roman Scotland* contains the encouraging phrase 'The head of the Moray Firth is the logical Roman objective.' Crawford, the first Archaeological Officer of the Ordnance Survey, was a pioneer of aerial photography and an associate of Alexander Keiller, and in the lean years after the war he cycled in the North searching for Romans and not only did he cross the Spey but he even investigated beyond Inverness.

On 1st March 1980 the Scottish Archaeological Forum held its 12th meeting and ten papers were presented devoted exclusively to *Agricola's Campaigns in Scotland* (1981). Only nine papers were published, but for a succinct appraisal of the state of knowledge at the time about Agricola and his campaigns in Scotland, this small volume is hard to beat. *The Northern Frontiers of Roman* by David J. Breeze (1982) is strong on Hadrian's and Antonine's walls and allocates the marching camps at Raedykes, Normandykes, Kintore, Ythanwells and Muiryfold to Severus, with only the smaller camps at Ythanwells and Auchinhove being classed as Agricolan. Hanson and Maxwell (1983), in their *Rome's North West Frontier*, produced the first study of the Antonine wall since Sir George

MacDonald (1934) published the second edition of *The Roman Wall in Scotland*. In Gordon Maxwell's (1989) *The Romans in Scotland* the author, while mentioning Mons Graupius, and extolling the virtues of William Roy, devotes most of his book to a thorough exposition and analysis of the Roman presence in lowland Scotland. If Maxwell somewhat neglects the north in his *The Romans in Scotland*, he handsomely makes up for it by devoting a whole volume to *A Battle Lost: Romans and Caledonians at Mons Graupius* (Maxwell 1990). Unlike Breeze, he allocates a Flavian (Agricolan) date to Normandykes, Kintore and Muiryfold, and after reviewing the evidence, antiquarian and modern, comes down in favour of the site, originally proposed by J. K. St. Joseph, at Bennachie. *Agricola and the conquest of the North* (Hanson 1991), is a good reference volume where the sizes of camps etc. are carefully tabulated in both hectares and acres and, in the obligatory map of Roman camps, arcing from the Dee to the Spey, no assumptions are made as to which dynasty they were built under. Wolliscroft (2002) in his account of excavations along the Gask ridge in *The Roman Frontier on the Gask Ridge, Perth and Kinross* does question the accepted wisdom that the fortlets and towers were constructed under Agricola and suggests that perhaps his predecessor Cerialis may have initiated this somewhat odd defence line. Finally, as cure for egocentricity, it is salutary to read *Rome and the North*, edited by Ellegård and Åkerström-Hougen (1996) which does not once mention Scotland.

This brief summary of modern writers has missed out many who are as equally worthy of being included. But just as there is difficulty in knowing where to start, there is an even greater difficulty in knowing where to stop. However there is one name which cannot be excluded and that is Professor Anne S. Robertson, excavator, teacher, writer and numismatist and one who quietly believed that it would only be a matter of time before the presence of Roman forts beyond the Spey would be established. Alas, she did not live to see and discuss the preliminary evidence, but her early encouragement remains as a warm memory.

References

Aubrey, J. *Monumenta Britannica* Vol. i, Sherbourne. 1982

Breeze, D.J. *The Northern Frontiers of Roman Britain*, London. 1982

Chalmers, G. *Caledonia*, Edinburgh. 1807, 1810, 1824

Crawford, O. G. S. *Topography of Roman Scotland*, Cambridge. 1949

Ellegård, C. & Åkerström-Hougen, G. eds. *Rome and the North*, Jonsered, Sweden. 1996

Frere, S. *Britannia - A History of Roman Britain*, London. 1987

Hanson, W. & Maxwell, G. *Rome's North West Frontier*, Edinburgh. 1983

Hanson, W. *Agricola and the Conquest of the North*, London. 1991

Horsley, J. *Britannia Romana*, London. 1733

Jameson, J. *Remarks on the Progress of the Roman Army in Scotland*, London. 1786

Kenworthy, J. ed. 'Agricola's Campaigns in Scotland' in *Scottish Archaeological Forum* No. 12. 1981

MacDonald, G. 'The Agricolan Occupation of North Britain' in *JRS* Vol. ix, London. 1919

MacDonald, G. *The Roman Wall in Scotland*, Edinburgh. 1934

Maxwell, G. *The Romans in Scotland*, Edinburgh. 1989

Maxwell, G. *A Battle Lost: Romans and Caledonians at Mons Graupius*, Edinburgh. 1990

Müller, C. *Ptolemaei Geographiae*, Paris. 1883-1901

NSA, New Statistical Account, Edinburgh. 1835-1844

OSA, Old Statistical Account of Scotland, Edinburgh. 1791-8

Pryce, T. D. & Birley, E. 'The Fate of Agricola's Northern Conquests' in *JRS* Vol. xxviii, London. 1938

Roy, W. 'The Military Antiquities of the Romans' in *North Britain*, London. 1793

St. Joseph, J. K. *Air Reconnaissance of North Britain* in *JRS* Vol. xli, London. 1951

Stuart, R. *Caledonia Romana*, Edinburgh. 1845

Wooliscroft, D. J. *The Roman Frontier on the Gask Ridge, Perth and Kinross*, Oxford. 2002

Chapter IV
The Imperial Roman Army

The Roman army, headquartered in Rome, existed for a thousand years from about 600BC to AD400 and during this time its weapons and tactics went through considerable changes. So, to simplify the discussion, the army will be looked at as it existed around AD100 when the Roman Empire was at its apogee. In the British Army the basic unit is the regiment. Each regiment has its flag, or colours, and in earlier days those disorientated in battle would look for the flag and rally round it. To a soldier the regiment is his father and mother, and a good soldier would rather die than dishonour his regiment. In the Roman army the fundamental infantry unit was the legion, with the eagle as its symbol, and where the eagle went, there the legionaries followed. However, most of the fighting was carried out by the auxiliaries or native troops; the legions, like all expensive weapons, were only used as a last resort.

By the year AD100 there were thirty legions, each containing ten cohorts, with each cohort consisting of six centuries. A quick calculation shows that each legion had 10 x 6 x 100 = 6,000 men. But the quick calculation is wrong, because despite the name, there were only 80 men per century and the first cohort had five double centuries. So the amended calculation is now (5 x 2 x 80) + (9 x 6 x 80) = 5120. But this is only the 'paper' strength because, in reality, there would be some who were sick, others on leave, perhaps a deserter or two, while others might be on detachment. Additional to the Roman infantry, each legion had some 120 cavalry; scouts, despatch riders, mounts for the officers etc. and for each squad of eight men or *contubernium* there was a mule or mule-drawn cart to carry their tent and corn quern etc. Finally there were the animals which drew the artillery. Vegetius (1993:60) states that there were 55 bolt-firing carriage ballistas and 10 mangonels or

Legionary Defensive Equipment *(not to scale)*

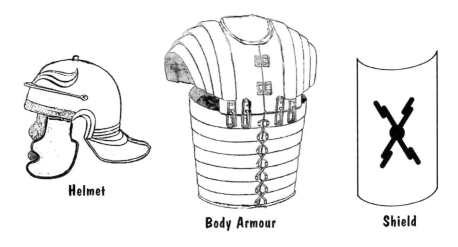

Helmet

Body Armour   Shield

Auxiliary (Cavalry) Defensive Equipment *(not to scale)*

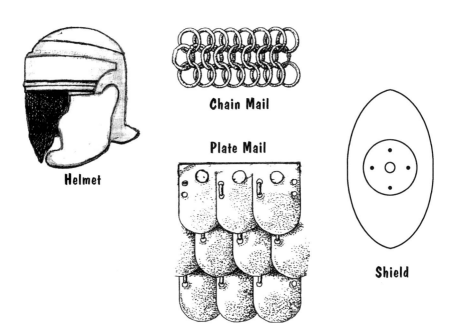

Chain Mail

Plate Mail

Helmet

Shield

Figure 6: Defensive Equipment - Legionary and Auxiliary (Cavalry)

onagers per legion. According to Marsden (1999:86), the latter could hurl a shot for over 200 metres. Although many legionaries were skilled craftsmen there must have been an additional need for farriers, blacksmiths and grooms. A legion, up to strength and on the march, must have been composed of about 6,000 men with some 1,250 animals (Peddie 1994:50).

A major source of information on the army and the equipment of the individual soldier is provided by the extraordinarily detailed sculpture on Trajan's column in Rome. Marcus Ulpius Nerva Trajanus (AD53 - 117), better known as Trajan, was emperor from AD98 to his death in AD117. He campaigned in Dacia, Armenia and Parthia and travelled down the Tigris to what is now known as the Persian Gulf. He initiated the construction of many new buildings in Rome and erected the magnificent column now named after him and which illustrates and glorifies several of his campaigns.

The legionary was equipped with a *galea*, originally a skin helmet, but the name had long since been applied to a metal helmet with neck and cheek guards *[Figure 6]*. A large rectangular shield, colourly decorated, known as a *scutum*, and curved to go partially round the body added to the soldier's protection. The *scutum* had a grooved rim of iron or bronze, and this enabled the shields to interlock to form a *testudo* or tortoise. The soldier's protection was completed by the *lorica segmentata* which covered the upper body with thin flexible sheets of iron. This was heavy but effective, and must have been a misery to keep rust-free in Britain. Just as in modern warfare the rifle is the soldier's best friend, so in the Roman army the *gladius* or short sword was the legionary's best friend. This was by design a very close-combat stabbing weapon. The grand gesture by the slashing swordsman may look magnificent, but the quick stab to the vitals is much more effective. As Vegetius (1993:13) writes, 'Romans ...easily beat those fighting with the edge, ...as a cut, whatever its force, seldom kills, because the vitals are protected by both armour and bones. But a stab driven two inches in is fatal; for necessarily

whatever goes in penetrates the vitals.' The sword was kept in a scabbard
on the right waist but strangely enough, Josephus (1959:379) contradicts
all other evidence by claiming that the sword was slung on the left. This
was a practice reserved for officers. The legionary carried his *pugio* or
dagger on the left. Another offensive weapon was the *pilum* or javelin
which was cunningly modified by Caesar. He had only the blade
tempered and left the shank untempered where it joined the shaft. If
the blade hit flesh it would sink in but if it hit a shield or hard ground
then the soft iron shank bent and the weapon became useless for throwing
back. Each legionary carried two *pila*. In addition to his weapons the
legionary carried a pick, an entrenching tool, saw, basket, a couple of
stakes or *pila muralia*, water bottle and at least three days' rations, though
this might be increased to seventeen days if marching through hostile
territory. His normal load of weapons, armour and rations could amount
to 60 pounds and this was the weight he was expected to carry on practice
route marches etc. How much was carried by transport is a matter of
conjecture. Presumably the tent and the quern were carried by cart or
mule, and if the troops were marching light then these, along with the
artillery, would be left behind and the soldiers would rely on emergency
rations such as pre-baked bread and biscuit.

Like all good armies, the Romans were sticklers for discipline and
drill, and there is some evidence from Vegetius and other writers that
the relaxation of discipline could lead to defeat in battle. There is no
doubt that a well-disciplined troop has a higher morale and increased
fighting efficiency compared to an ill-disciplined mob. The efforts of
the sergeant-majors and centurions on the parade ground were always
justified when their trainees went into battle. Vegetius (1993:4) comments
that the best recruits come from the country and this is confirmed by a
story from our own time. In the 1939/40 phoney war the Argyll and
Sutherland Highlanders were in the front line in France overlooking a
German position. One company of the Highlanders was composed of
ghillies, shepherds and farmers from the rural areas while the other
company had recruited from the towns of Central Scotland. When the

latter was on duty there were alarms and excursions every night. Flares arced into the sky and there was the odd rattle of Bren gun fire. When the country folk took over, everybody, except those on duty, could have a good night's sleep. All was peace and quiet. Bushes in the moonlight no longer metamorphosed into Germans creeping towards the British lines.

Although the legions of Rome receive the most attention, the bulk of the fighting was carried out by the *auxilia* or native troops. There were archers from Syria, stone slingers from the Balearic Islands and horsemen from North Africa. The *auxilia* were not Roman citizens, but received citizenship on honourable discharge from the service. According to Webster (1969:144), some 5,000 ex-soldiers were made Romans every year. If the average length of service was 25 years and 50% never made it through to retiral, then there must have been between 125,000 and 250,000 *auxilia* in service at any one time throughout the empire. *Auxilia* were organised in units of five hundred or a thousand, divided into centuries, which were only 80 strong (Watson 1969:15 Davies 1989:141)

The Romans sat uncomfortably on horseback and preferred to recruit horses and horsemen from all over the Empire who brought with them their terminology and techniques of fighting, so there is not the same standardisation of the cavalry as there is for the Roman legions. The organisation of the cavalry is thus somewhat obscure, but nominally they were organised in a troop or *ala milliaria* numbering 1,000 men but, like a military *century*, having a lower actual strength of 768. The *ala milliaria* was divided into twenty-four *turmae* of thirty troopers with an additional two officers, the *duplicarius* and the *sesquiplicarius*. Each cavalryman was equipped with a much longer sword than the infantry, a helmet and a round shield, and some wore chain mail. Stirrups not having yet been invented, their saddles were deep with substantial back and front rests to prevent the rider sliding backwards when he thrust at the enemy with his *hasta* or spear. Cavalry training was absolutely essential for the efficient functioning of this arm of the service, and this training was codified in AD136 by Flavius Arrianus Xenophon otherwise known to us as Arrian (Hyland 1993:3). We do not know if the individual cavalryman travelled with a remount or what arrangements were made for the supply and retraining of horses to replace those killed or wounded during a campaign.

But more than horses could be wounded, and we know that the Romans employed mainly Greek doctors, though the organisation of moving injured men from the battlefield to field or base hospital is not known. It seems most unlikely that a wounded soldier would be placed in a cart and then driven several hundreds of miles to a base camp. What is more likely is that the wounded were taken to the coast and shipped out by the nearest naval unit. The campaign under Agricola was very much a combined operation, involving close co-operation between the navy and army as has been well described by Martin (1992:1-34).

In considering the movement of the Roman army in the north-east we have to realise that the army did not consist of a self-sufficient group of legions who built neat symmetrical camps along their route of march but, additional to the legions, was a large number of auxiliaries, carts, mules, medical orderlies, grooms, wagoners etc., all requiring rations, shelter and room to park their gear.

In considering the number of men who could be accommodated in assorted sizes of Roman camps, few commentators have considered the needs of the *auxilia* or the requirements of the pack animals and the carts and artillery. Carts and artillery take up space while animals need both space and time to forage. Peddie (1994:42-79), having learnt to handle mules in Burma, is one of the few to appreciate the practical logistics of handling men and animals on active service. There are also problems of living in a ridge tent which the summer time camper is not liable to experience. Roy (1793:41-77) spent much of his earlier days in tents so his observations on the castramentation of the Romans is well worthy of consideration. However, as he ruefully admits, 'The distribution of the several parts of the Roman camp admits of some difficulties, and has occasioned much controversy among the curious.' Roy, in his analysis of Roman camps, leans heavily on Polybius (c.204 - 122BC), a Greek historian who was taken as a prisoner to Rome where he wrote his famous history, which has come down to us only in fragmentary form. Initially, when quoting dimensions, Roy does not make it clear whether he is using Roman or imperial feet and it is only towards the end of his treatise that he converts the overall dimensions of the camp into imperial measurement. The Roman foot = 11.6 ins imperial and to avoid further confusion all subsequent measurements will be assumed to be imperial and calculation to metric can be carried out using the following factors.

Feet to metres, x by 0.3048   *Acres to hectares, x by 0.4047*

Metres to feet, x by 3.281   *Hectares to acres, x by 2.471*

For those somewhat removed in time from when they knew what a rod, pole or perch was, the following aide-mémoire may be useful.

3 feet = 1 yard

4840 sq. yards = 1 acre

10,000 sq. metres= 1 hectare

After somewhat confusingly describing how a presumed two-legion marching camp is set out, Roy eventually declares that the outer rampart comprises a rectangle of sides 2,077 and one third feet and a dead space of 193.25ft between rampart and the core of the camp. This 193.25ft imperial is the equivalent of 200ft Roman and for simplicity in subsequent calculation this latter figure will be used. This dead ground varied in total area with the size of camp, but the critical dimension of width did not vary and was always 200ft.

In considering the number of troops associated with a particular size of camp, there are few facts and many assumptions. Initial assumptions, without documentary evidence, are that the legions travelled with *auxilia,* who were tented on the scale of the legions. A further assumption is that the IXth Legion had a predilection for *clavicula* type gates and could thus be associated with the camps at Stracathro, Ythanwells (smaller camp) and Auchinhove, with an average area of 35 acres each. Thus one legion requires 35 acres; two legions take up 70 acres and three legions require 100+ acres and thus fit snugly into the area profiles of Normandykes (106 acres), Ythanwells (111 acres – larger camp) and Muiryfold (109 acres). Unfortunately, this simplistic arithmetic is faulty.

The single-legion camp takes up 35 acres, measured round the top of the rampart which has a single side length of 411.6 yards. The dead ground measures 200ft across, so the inner core of the camp, in which all the troops, horses, wagons and altars have to be housed, amounts to 28 acres. To accommodate eight men comfortably you need a minimum tent size of 15 ft x 15ft. Peddie (1994:46) reckons that a centurion would have a tent of 20 ft x 20ft, simply for himself. Senior officers would, no doubt, have expected even more lavish accommodation. Unfortunately it has not been possible to confirm these dimensions. Davies (1989:88), quoting Hyginus, gives the tent dimensions for an eight man unit as 'ten feet square plus an extra two feet for the guy ropes.' Neither Goldsworthy (1998), or Le Bohec (1994) give tent dimensions. But Webster (1969:167) gives not only dimensions but a diagram, in accordance with Hyginus, as reconstructed by I. A. Richmond. According to Webster, 'Their measurements inclusive of guy-ropes being ten Roman feet square.' The Roman foot was slightly smaller than the imperial but even ten foot x ten foot, imperial, is a miserably small allowance for eight men, complete with armour and weapons. If each man takes up a space 3ft x 6ft then eight men fully occupy 12 ft x 12 ft which, from experience, is comfortable for four, possible with six and very difficult indeed with eight. Some have argued that the tents were only intended to shelter six, as two from the *contubernium* would be on fatigues or guard duty. But this is most unlikely, as an army cannot function efficiently if 25% of the force are continuously on duty. At times 100% will require to be in action, but these are for limited periods only.

However, it is apparent from the evidence that the Roman legionary was prepared to put up with conditions that a modern serviceman would find intolerable. In 1987, R. Birley excavated enough of a Roman tent at Vindolanda to make a reconstruction possible (Driel-Murray 1989:367-372). The reconstruction confirms the 10ft square floor dimensions but an associated diagram shows the tents pitched impossibly close, while a further diagram by Driel-Murray shows how eight men could be squeezed into the tent, with six lying side by side and two at their feet, but this leaves little room for turning over, let alone space for baggage and armour. The basic tent was 10ft x 10ft, and Roman feet at that, but a tent needs guy ropes and so an additional 2ft all round has been allocated to accommodate them. Then you need space between the tents: not only for access without falling foul of guy ropes, but to act as a fire break and allow of drainage ditches – something absolutely essential in Scotland. A minimum of 3ft would appear to be essential. Then there is the space in front of the tent. Here the legionaries would pile their arms and armour, cook their meal and have access to their muster station. A minimum of 14ft x 8ft, clear of all guy ropes, is required, and this gives a grand total of 374 sq. ft or 42 sq. yards per *contubernium* [Figure 7].

Of the 28 acres theoretically available to the troops, let us arbitrarily allocate 50% to the officers, shrines, horse lines etc. This leaves 14 acres, and allowing 42 square yards and eight men per *contubernium* there is room for 8,400 soldiers, which is conveniently close to the accepted strength of a legion with its associated *auxilia* and cavalry. Let us now look at the dimensions for a camp three times the size of the assumed single-legion 35-acre site. The size of such a camp would be 105 acres which gives a single side rampart length of 713 yards and a core camp

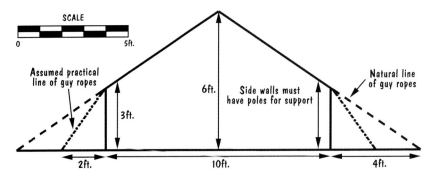

Roman Tent after van Driel-Murray (1989) *[modified]*

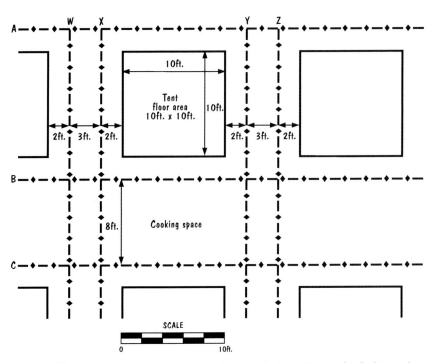

Spacing of Roman tents to allow for guy ropes, drainage ditches and space for Cooking and passage between tents. Total area required per *contubernium* = **374 sq. ft.**

Figure 7: Roman Tent Space

size of 69.5 acres, and allowing 50% to the officers etc. this still leaves space for 32,000 troops. Thus, whatever errors there are in the initial assumptions, it appears that trebling the overall size of a camp almost quadruples the number of soldiers it can contain.

According to Maxwell (1990:52), the area of the Roman camps at Raedykes, Normandykes, Kintore, Ythanwells and Muiryfold, when converted to acres, averages out at 106 acres, an area of ample space to contain four legions with auxiliaries. Logie Durno, facing Bennachie, is 144 acres, and this must raise the question whether it is reasonable to continue the speculation that it is of Flavian date. When it was originally discovered by J. K. St. Joseph he allocated it to the activities of Severus, and it was only later (St. Joseph 1978:271-287) that he proposed that not only was it Flavian but was the site of the battle of Mons Graupius. There are difficulties in consigning Durno to either the Flavian or Severan period. If the camps leading up to Durno from the Dee are Flavian, from whence came the Severan troops to fill the 144 acres of Durno? If Flavian, and its spacing between Kintore and Ythanwells is suggestive, then why the size sufficient to hold up to six legions? Numbers not usually associated with Agricola. If Durno is Severan then there must be a 100-acre Flavian camp either near or under the known camp. Until the camps stretching from Aberdeen towards Moray [Figure 8] are all dated, it may be somewhat pointless to speculate who did what to whom and where and when. However, the recent discovery of more bread ovens at Kintore (Hunter 2004:266), increases the possibility that here may be the actual point where the Flavian legions started marching light into enemy territory as described by Tacitus. If we ever are to solve the mystery of the Romans in the north, it will be necessary to speculate, but with caution. It may be that the 100-acre camps represent some as yet unrecognised Roman expedition while the Flavian presence is provided in the shape of the few 30-acre camps still discernible, such as the ones at Ythanwells, Auchinhove and Bellie. Auchinhove may provide a clue as to why there are so few smaller Roman camps to be found in east Banffshire and Moray. St. Joseph (1951:65), describing

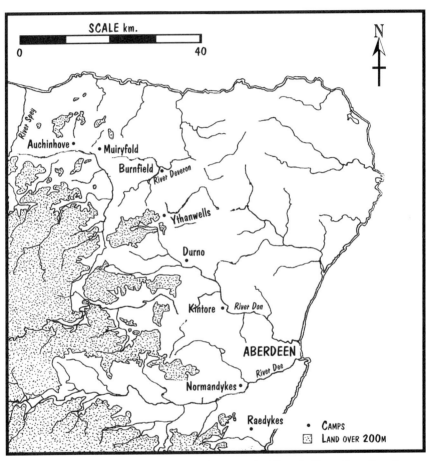

Figure 8: Putative Flavian Camps in North-East Scotland

Auchinhove, makes it clear that he was only able to see one side with a curved north-east corner. The site has been examined for over thirty-five years since then and flown over several times and a crop mark has never again been seen. It may be that within a generation, a crop mark which had survived since Roman times, has been lost for ever. How many more are there?

The Roman army under Agricola, wherever it camped, brought the Caledonian tribes to battle and, using better discipline and tactics against superior numbers, achieved a notable victory, or at least so said Tacitus, who just happened to be Agricola's son-in-law and thus not necessarily an unbiased reporter. The battle took place at Mons Graupius, an alleged rounded hill, presumably fronting a plain where the fighting occurred. Scotland is full of such places and early antiquarians and modern scholars have spilt more ink on the site of the battle than blood was lost during it. Maxwell (1990), in his *A Battle Lost*, covers the historical ground very effectively before homing in on his favoured site of Bennachie. Among the historians whom he mentions is Feacham (1970:120-4) who suggested Duncrub, near the Tay and Earn, could be the Mons Graupius of legend, particularly as there is a philological link between the words *crub* and *graup*. Accepting this link then perhaps we should examine more closely Crùban Mór and Cruban Beag, which are hills just lying to the west of the A9 not far north of Dalwhinnie and some ten kilometres from the great fortress of Dun da Lamh which dominates the whole of upper Strathspey, while between the A9 and the A889 road to Spean Bridge lies the wide flat lands of the Càthar Mòr. Watson (1926:232) tells us that *Cathair* means 'fort' and that *Cathair Mhaothail* 'Muthil Fort' was the old name for the Roman fort at Ardoch.

However, before we become too obsessed with the alleged correlation between *crup, crub* and rounded hills, Breeze (2002:305-311) cogently argues that *Graupius* might be *Craupius* and thus could be connected with Welsh *crib* meaning comb. Bennachie, when viewed from the east along the A96, in the words of Breeze: 'Its outline of four peaks along an east-west ridge thus resembles a comb for hair or the comb of a cock. A Brittonic name in *Crip-* 'comb: bird's crest' thus suits it admirably, as it suits no other mountain at locations proposed for the battle of Mons Graupius.' While the argument is attractive, it is a matter of observation that the Cruben hills on the A9 are even more jagged than the crest of Bennachie.

An appreciation of the battle of Mons Graupius has been carried out by Bartlam (1999:1-22) in which he uses his own skills as a former army planning officer to consider not only the tactics of the battle but the problems of supply on both sides, and he also draws on his own experience as a yacht skipper when he discusses the contribution of the fleet. Like St. Joseph and Maxwell, Bartlam choses Bennachie as the site for the battle, and he makes light of the difficulty presented by the Urie burn by proposing that the actual battle field was more to the east on reasonably well drained flat ground.

However, if we believe Henderson (1984:23-8) we should be looking for Mons Graupius far beyond Inverness. Like most investigators he starts by examining the work of his predecessors and it is not until he comes to his penultimate page and almost to the end of his article that he states 'Agricola fought Calgacus in the 'last wedge' – ie. Sutherland, or Caithness – and that he returned to the south of Scotland by the one major route through the Highlands, namely the Great Glen.' Henderson's whole article is a cry for the experts to raise their eyes from the satisfying shibboleths of the familiar and to look about them and examine the unfamiliar without prejudice.

We do know that the Roman army, on at least one occasion, marched through North-East Scotland to the Spey. With our present knowledge we can only make a guess as to the age of the camps. It is reasonable to assume that if the Romans reached the Spey, then they crossed it, if only to visit the *polis* of *Tuesis* and the fort at *Pinnata Castra*. There would be other, more pressing strategic reasons to advance, reasons which have already been discussed in Chapter I. This advance into Moray could be either pre or post Mons Graupius and, again, we can only hypothesise. What is more reasonable to accept are the two statements by Tacitus (1967:117-8), *in fines Borestorum totum exercitum deducit* and *quo novarum gentium animi ipsa transitus mora terrerentur, in hibernis locavit.* The first statement implies that the Roman army was on higher ground and went down *(deducit)* to the land of the Boresti. However, Wolfson (2002) argues that *Borestorum* is a textual corruption of *in finis boreos totum deducit,* 'He led his entire army down into the northern extremities.' The second states that the army moved slowly and deliberately, the better to terrorise the tribes, to its winter quarters. These quarters could have been at Inchtuthil or even York. But what is more significant, though not stated by Tacitus, is that forts with auxiliary troops most probably would have been left in the newly conquered territories. The Roman subjection and consequent occupation of Wales serves as an example. No sane general captures ground and then withdraws, unless it is for a greater strategic reason, and that reason did not occur until two years of occupation had passed. If Wolfson's argument is accepted, then we must look for the battle of Mons Graupius in the Highlands or at least on elevated ground with ready access to the sea.

As for the route back to base, when Agricola led his troops south, summer was well past. Post Mons Graupius he had to fix sites for forts and see his legionaries dig the minimum univallate defences. He had to select the auxiliary troops he was leaving behind and advise the officers how and where to contact the fleet and work out an emergency plan in the, however unlikely, event of the natives revolting. All this staff work would have taken several weeks before he was able to give the order to march. With time against him and a Highland winter about to close in, Agricola had three choices in his route south. He could take the long flat way back through Aberdeen and Strathmore etc. or he could take the water route down the Great Glen, but if he did this, and his intention was to head for Inchtuthil, then he had to cross over some very desolate and very high country from what is now Fort William to the east coast. There is a third choice, which is the one taken by most modern travellers, and that is the A9 which runs from Inverness to Perth. However, if Agricola did use this route then he took one of the earlier variants, known as Comyn's Road which runs between Badenoch and Blair Atholl and this will be discussed later.

The army which Agricola deployed at the battle of Mons Graupius probably consisted of three legions. In Britain he had four legions at his disposal, *II Augusta* stationed at Caerleon, the *IX Hispana* at York, *II Adiutrix* at Chester and, intended for Inchtuthil, the *XX Valeria Victrix*. However, it would have been a very bold or rash general who committed all his army to the field and left no strategic reserve in the event of trouble arising elsewhere. None of these legions could have been up to strength. Headquarters staff with the necessary guard personnel must have been left at base while units had been detached for service in Dacia. Then there was the usual attrition due to sickness and wounds. It would be a fortunate legion that could muster 4,000 combat troops, and a better estimate might be 3,500. The *auxilia*, who would do the bulk of the fighting, numbered in total about 8,000 men, supported by 4,000 cavalry, giving a grand force of 22,500. It must be emphasised that this figure is hypothetical and, while it may have been smaller, it was unlikely to have been larger. According to Tacitus, opposing them was a much larger mob. It would be wrong to refer to it as an army; as the term army implies some sort of discipline and coherence. As far as we know, these were qualities somewhat lacking in the first-century Caledonians. Again, according to Tacitus, the Romans were vastly outnumbered by the Caledonians, but, as somebody said in another context, 'he would, (say that) wouldn't he!'

As regards the size of the mob we have only the word of Tacitus to go on. After the battle he claims that 10,000 of the enemy fell while earlier he had noted that Agricola was greatly outnumbered. Allowing for the victor's normal exaggeration it would not be unreasonable to assume that the Caledonians numbered at least 30,000 fighting men with the same number of associated family and camp followers. So, somewhere in Scotland in AD83 or AD84 there was assembled some 60,000 people, and – and here we are reduced to guesswork – perhaps 500 chariots with 1,000 ponies, complete with an entourage of blacksmiths with portable forges, a supply of charcoal and, most important of all, adequate rations to feed man and beast for at least a few days. A good daily ration for an animal is about 10 kilograms of dry fodder a day while an active human prefers 1.5 kilos but can exist on 1 kilo of grain or 0.5 kilo of meat. While individually this ration is quite modest, when multiplied by the numbers requiring to be fed it means that every day the Caledonians were consuming sixty tonnes of grain while their animals were eating another ten. Even considering that in the first century AD people were capable of living on very meagre supplies so that their ration was only half that considered essential today, it still means that every day the countryside around the gathering had to supply 35 tonnes of food. Thus the requirements for fodder and rations makes the hill of Bennachie, rising above the extensive surrounding arable and pastoral landscape of Aberdeenshire, a strong candidate for the site of Mons Graupius.

To raise such a large gathering from tribes which, we assume, were not always on the friendliest of terms, indicates that their leader Calgacus was a very special individual indeed. He must have had access to a supra-tribal organisation and the only candidate for that must be the Druids. Druidism had been forbidden in Gaul by both the emperors Tiberius and Claudius and the surviving Druids fled to *Mona* (Anglesey) where the Romans pursued them in AD61 and cut down their sacred groves. When Anglesey was destroyed it would be natural for the surviving Druids to flee north to escape the Roman legions, and when these legions eventually pursued them north, the Druids, with their first-hand experience, would be the natural agitators and organisers of the resistance.

The Caledonians held the high ground while the Romans assembled on the plain. Auxiliary infantry in the centre, cavalry on the flanks, with the legions assembled in the centre immediately behind the auxiliaries. As the Caledonians moved to outflank the Romans, Agricola thinned his line and extended it, so much so that his senior officers suggested that the legions be deployed in battle formation, but Agricola continued with his extension. If he had 8,000 front line auxiliary troops and initially marshalled them six deep, then his line, originally 1.3km long, was ultimately extended to about 2.5km, but dangerously thin, being only three men deep.

The battle started with the Caledonian chariots rattling between the lines, exchanging missiles with the Romans as they rushed along. By this time, chariots were somewhat passé elsewhere but were still high tech in the Highlands. Their use raises many questions which have rarely been asked, let alone answered. Was there a supply depot for the chariots where tyres could be fitted to wheels and the horses fed and groomed? And how was the necessary fodder collected and transported to the ponies? After an exchange of missiles the Caledonian foot warriors started to move downhill and Agricola gave the order for four cohorts of Batavians and two cohorts of Tungrians to advance and attack. The Batavians came from what is now Holland while the Tungrians were raised in Belgium and their total number would amount to about one third of the line where, presumably, they occupied the centre. These soldiers were trained to push with their shields and stab with their swords. Their opponents came howling and slashing, but before the slash could connect, the Caledonian sword bearer suffered a fatal jab to his vitals. The same tactics were used by the followers of Prince Charles Edward Stuart at Culloden and failed equally miserably against the bayonets of the Redcoats. At the critical moment, and here timing was all, Agricola ordered his cavalry to sweep round and attack the enemy from the rear. For long seconds the battle hung in the balance and then the Caledonians broke and started to run, while the Roman cavalry went pig-sticking with homo sapiens as the pigs. Tacitus claimed that one Roman, a subaltern by the name of Aulus Atticus, was killed, while the auxiliaries, infantry and cavalry, suffered 360 dead and, no doubt, many more wounded. The Caledonians allegedly suffered losses of about 10,000, but even allowing for natural victorious exaggeration the total may well have run into several thousands. 'Twas a famous victory' and after the battle the dead would be stripped of any valuables and armour, prisoners and hostages would be shackled, and after a few days of rest the army would have been on the move again, down to meet the fleet, embark the wounded and the prisoners, draw fresh rations and generally relax for a few days.

The time for rest would not have been long. While the auxiliaries sorted out their kit and sharpened their swords, Agricola, with his staff officers and detachments of legionaries, would have been inspecting the countryside and establishing fort sites, which the accompanying legionaries would immediately start to construct. As time was short only the bare essentials such as a ditch and defended gateway were built, while the auxiliaries may well have been expected to spend their first winter in tents or wattle and daub huts. The forts garrisoned, the legions could then march south as mentioned earlier.

References

Bartlam, W. A. *De Proelio ad Montem Graupium*, Elgin. 1999 (unpublished)

Breeze, A. 'Philology on Tacitus's Graupian Hill and Trucculan Harbour' in *PSAS* Vol. 132. 2002

Davies, R. *Service in the Roman Army*, Edinburgh. 1989

Driel-Murray, C. V. 'A Roman Tent: Vindolanda Tent 1' in *Roman Frontier Studies*, Exeter. 1989

Feacham, R. W. 'Mons Graupius = Duncrub?' in *Antiquity* Vol. 44. 1970

Goldsworthy, A. K. *The Roman Army at War 100BC - AD200*, Oxford. 1998

Henderson, A. R. 'From 83 to 1983: *On the Trail of Mons Graupius'* in *The Deeside Field* Vol. 18, Aberdeen. 1984

Hunter, F. '*Roman Britain-Scotland'* in *Britannia* Vol. xxxv. 2004

Hyland, A. *Training the Roman Cavalry*, Stroud. 1993

Josephus, F. *The Jewish Wars*, Penguin. 1959

Le Bohec, Y. *The Imperial Roman Army*, London. 1994

Marsden, E. W. *Greek & Roman Artillery*, Oxford. 1999

Martin, C. 'Water Transport and the Roman Occupations of North Britain' in *Scotland and the Sea*, ed. Smout, T. C., Edinburgh. 1992

Maxwell, G. *A Battle Lost: Romans and Caledonians at Mons Graupius*, Edinburgh. 1990

Peddie, J. *The Roman War Machine*, Stroud. 1994

Roy, W. *The Military Antiquities of the Romans in North Britain*, London. 1793

St. Joseph, J. K. 'Air Reconnaisance of North Britain' in *JRS* Vol. xli. 1951

St. Joseph, J. K. 'The Camp at Durno and Mons Graupius' in *Britannia* Vol. ix. 1978

Taciti, C. ed., Ogilvie, R. M. & Richmond, I. *De Vita Agricola*, Oxford. 1967

Vegetius ed. Milner, N. P. *Epitome of Military Science*, Liverpool. 1993

Watson, G. R. *The Roman Soldier*, Thames & Hudson. 1969

Watson, W. J. *History of the Celtic Place-Names of Scotland*, Edinburgh. 1926

Webster, G. *The Roman Imperial Army*, London. 1969

Wolfson, S. *The Boresti: The Creation of a Myth*, 2002, http://myweb.tiscali.co.uk/fartherlands/appendix.htm

CHAPTER V
The Imperial Roman Navy and *Trucculensis Portus*

It is an odd fact that for every book published on the Roman navy there are at least a hundred on the Roman army. The standard work on the Roman navy first appeared in 1941 and the third edition is still in print, (Starr:1993), and it was only in 2003 that a book specifically referring to Roman Britain and the Roman navy was published, (Mason:2003). In addition there are papers published in various journals, the most comprehensive being by Martin (1992:1-34), but the total is still meagre compared to the torrent of writing about the army. Then there is the site of *Trucculensis Portus*, the harbour to which the Agricolan fleet returned to after the battle of Mons Graupius. As Tacitus (1967:118) succinctly puts it, *Trucculensem portum tenuit*. This unlocated harbour has been moved about Great Britain, from the south coast of England to Montrose and from Sutherland round Cape Wrath to south-west Scotland and across to Skye. Perhaps we should heed the advice of Wolfson (2002) who maintains that *Trucculensem* is hopelessly corrupted and the passage should read *et simul classis secunda tempestate ac fama trux Tulensem portum tenuit* which translates as: 'And at the same time the fleet, its ruthlessness enhanced by rumour and favourable weather, reached Shetland harbour.'

In writing of the penultimate campaign of Agricola, Tacitus (1967:108-109) describes how the war was pushed forward simultaneously by land and sea, commenting that the army and marines would often meet in the same camps where they would exchange accounts of experiences and, although Tacitus does not mention it, such boasting may well have degenerated into internecine brawling. Tacitus also mentions that intelligence from prisoners revealed that the natives were alarmed and despondent by the appearance of the Roman fleet.

While Rome was still a city state she had no need for a fleet, but consequent territorial expansion led her into conflict with Carthage, the great trading nation on the other side of the Mediterranean. Carthage had a navy and when Rome drifted into the first Punic war in 264BC the Romans had to hire vessels from the Greeks. The Romans however did not adopt any recognised naval tactics from anybody, but developed their own, based on their disciplined infantry. They designed grappling devices to hold an enemy vessel to one of their own ships and then poured soldiers into the shackled ship. Their tactics were eventually successful and by 240BC the Roman navy ruled supreme in the Mediterranean though, according to some commentators, this had been at a cost of some 500 quinqueremes.

The quinquereme was the largest type of vessel afloat in ancient times. Allegedly developed by Dionysius of Syracuse in circa 400BC, it had five banks of oars on either side and with some 300 rowers it displaced some 90 tons and could carry 120 troops. If the quinquereme was the battleship of the ancient world then the trireme was the cruiser. It was a light craft of some 120ft long and 20ft in beam and carried 170 rowers, 10 marines and 20 sailors. Continuing the analogy with more recent war ships, the destroyer of the Roman fleet was the *liburna*. This fast and light vessel had 100 rowers in two banks, plus a mid sail and a fore sail. With a length of 100ft and a beam of 18ft, those deployed in northern waters were probably decked in order to afford the rowers some protection against the weather. According to Morrison and Coates (1986), pine wood was used for the planking and external woodwork while ash, elm and mulberry were used for stem and bow timbers. Pitch was used to coat the exterior, while wax and resin were also applied to help make the structure watertight.

In the days of the Empire there were several Roman fleets, but only the *Classis Britannica* need concern us here. The admiral of the fleet was a *praefectus* and was paid 100,000 *sesterces* a year (Mason 2003:27-29). Beneath the *praefectus* was the *subpraefectus* who commanded a squadron of ten ships and, under him was the *trierarchus* or ship's captain. The captain's mate or pilot was the *gubernator* but most of the ship's crew, with a few exceptions, were all army personnel, including the oarsmen who, when occasion demanded, would seize weapons and either attack or defend as required. Medical staff, clerks, and priests to examine the omens and advise the *trierarchus* were also part of the naval establishment. The names of a few of the *praefecti* have come down to us (Spaul 2002:47), but only two of the ships they commanded (Mason 2003:105), though we do know that names such as *Mars*, *Venus*, *Diana* and *Minerva* were popular.

The main northern fleet depot was at Boulogne, from where in AD43 the Emperor Claudius set sail to conquer Britain, and after his successful landfall the fleet base was transferred to Richborough (*Rutupiensem*). After some fifty years there as the main fleet harbour in Britain the Roman navy moved its base to Dover. Associated with its ship-repairing facilities at the dockyards was extensive iron-smelting in the Weald with major production centres at Bardon and Beauport Park. In any search for Roman harbours it may be useful to look for evidence of local iron-smelting.

After the battle of Mons Graupius, Agricola 'ordered his admiral to sail round the north of Britain' while meanwhile on land he took hostages and placed his army in winter quarters. At about the time he was completing his troop deployment, the fleet, which had been aided by favourable weather, returned to *Trucculensis Portus* from where it had started its voyage (Tacitus 1967:118). This casual comment by Tacitus is almost impossible to understand. Ogilvie and Richmond in Tacitus (1967:282), referring to *Trucculensem*, state: 'Both the name and the locality are unknown and the text is probably corrupt.'

In what little evidence we have, per Tacitus, it is clear that Agricola used the navy as part of a combined operation and there is no reason to think that he would allow the navy to disappear to some remote port over the winter, leaving the army to police the newly acquired territories.

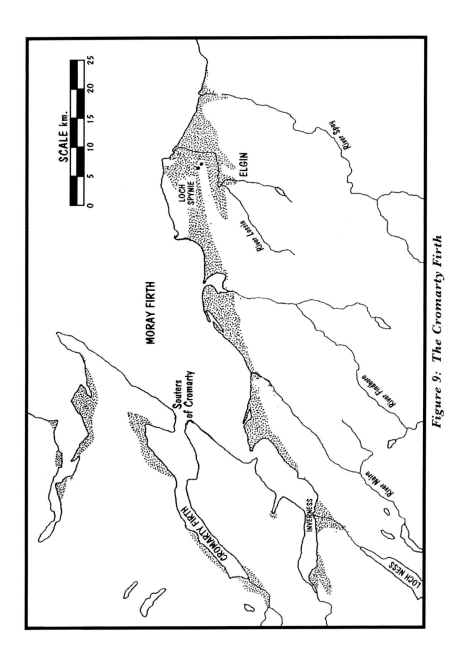

Figure 9: The Cromarty Firth

The navy had been instrumental in achieving victory and would be expected to take its part in the continuing peace-keeping. But the navy had also its own priorities. After a season at sea many of the ships would require to be overhauled, while the sailors would be looking for what is euphemistically termed rest and recreation. Agricola would want the navy to be based near his newly-won territories while the navy would require access to the following: Safe and secure anchorage with sandy beaches for careening. Timber, preferably substantial stands of pine with minor quantities of willow and hazel. Iron ore and a community able to supply beer and girls would complete the list of essential requirements.

The first essential requirement is a deep-water harbour able to shelter ships no matter from which direction the wind is blowing. The only completely safe harbour between Aberdeen and Thurso is the Cromarty Firth which sheltered the British Grand Fleet in two world wars *[Figure 9]*. From the Souters of Cromarty, which guard the entrance to this great natural harbour, you can look across into Moray and if a beacon sent a danger message then boats with marines could be across the Firth in four hours. Inside the harbour there are fine sandy beaches ideal for beaching and examining ships, while amongst the natural timber growing in the vicinity was pine, producing long and easily worked planks (Maclennan 1984:50, Steven & Carlisle 1959:36-38).

The requirement for iron ore would probably be met by bog iron but there is a source of high quality haematite, albeit now only present in small quantities, in the cliffs stretching between Rosemarkie and Cromarty (Ross 2003). According to the Keays (1994:199) Thomas Ross of Pitkerie established an iron works in Cromarty in the latter years of the 18th century but the ore for this was imported from Sweden, while Gillen (1984:38) notes that lead mines operated in Strath Glass in the first half of the 19th century. There are pockets of bitumen in the Old Red Sandstone (Ross 2003), but no evidence that these have ever been worked. However, it is worth recording that in the vicinity of the

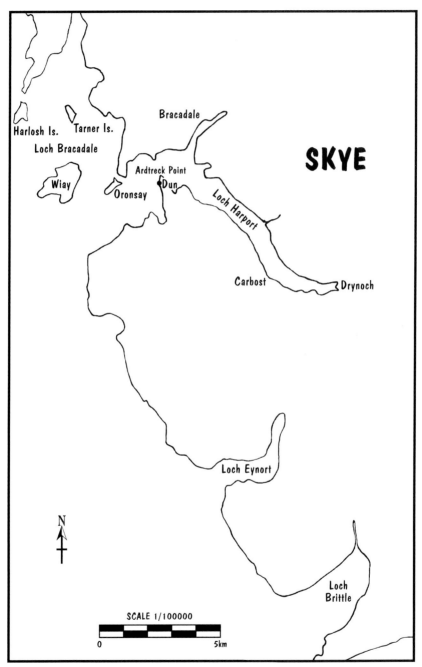

Figure 10: Loch Harport

Cromarty Firth are found all the basic necessities for fleet maintenance some two thousand years ago.

There are rival candidates for the site of *Trucculensis Portus*. Horsley (1733:App. 7A) equates it with *Ritupae* which is Richborough and this was the favoured association for the next two hundred years. Ogilvie and Richmond (1967: 282-3) continue this argument by suggesting that *Rutupensem* could well have been the original spelling and this leads neatly into Richborough. Reed (1971:147-148) shuffles the letters around to make *Ugrulentum* which appears in the *Ravenna* manuscript but is itself not very helpful as nobody knows the location of *Ugrulentum*. Hind (1974:285-8), again a wordsmith, favours the base word *Itunocelum* but this in no way assists in determining its location. Rivet and Smith (1979:479-480) are refreshingly honest and state: 'Since we cannot... be sure of the original form, we have no prospect of a solution. An attractive identification might be with Sandwood Loch (Sutherland)'. Jones and Mattingly (1990) in their *Atlas of Roman Britain* neatly solve the problem of the location of *Trucculensis Portus* by not mentioning the place.

Breeze (2002:305-311) continues the philology attack on *Trucculensis* and includes *Mons Graupius* in his offensive. He demolishes the long-accepted belief that *Graupius* can be linked to the Welsh *crwb* meaning a hump and postulates that it is cognate with *crib* or comb, and this is wonderfully descriptive of Bennachie as seen from the Aberdeen side. Turning his attention to *Trucculensis* he searches in the Brittonic vocabularies for words associated with break, cut, fissure etc. and finds plenty in Breton, Welsh and even Lithuanian. Armed with this new information he looks on the west coast of Scotland for places which are fissured or where the landscape is broken. This is a promising approach but, unfortunately, there are many candidates which meet the required criteria. Eventually Breeze comes down in favour of Loch Harport which is also strongly promoted as a candidate by MacKie (2000) using the excavations at Dun Ardtrek to advance his argument *[Figure 10]*. In the preamble to his paper MacKie makes the cogent observation: 'It is surely one of the more striking aspects of modern Scottish archaeology that those investigating the Roman military occupations of the south of the country and those studying the native populations the legions encountered rarely co-operate with one another and that their programmes of excavations, fieldwork and research largely exist in two separate worlds, published in separate journals and discussed at separate conferences.'

Dun Ardtrek is in Skye on a headland guarding the entrance to Loch Harport at NG335 357. According to MacKie it was built between 400BC and AD250. It had been subject to most ruthless treatment in that it had been fired, the entrance door had been battered inward and the heat was so great that some of the stones on the floor were vitrified. After the fire had subsided the upper part of the walls were razed, rendering the structure completely incapable of defence. Within the structure and, presumably in situ before the destruction, were a much corroded Roman iron axe hammer and shards of a fine Roman wheel-made vessel. Such items are rare on a native site and are indicative of Roman occupation or at least visitation. However evidence that the Roman fleet carried out a punitive expedition in Skye is not proof that the navy over-wintered in Loch Harport. Agricola had conquered new tribes in the east of Scotland and, in the event of any trouble, he would have wanted his fleet to be readily available to render assistance to the army if required. Even if a despatch rider could reach Skye in two days, it would take the fleet at least several days to reach the Moray Firth, and that is assuming that the tides through the Pentland Firth were favourable. If the fleet were stationed in the Cromarty Firth and was alerted by beacon or torch, then it could be off the Moray coast in a few hours. Breeze's argument that *Trucculensis* took its name from a breach in the landscape is exemplified by the gash in the landscape which leads into the safe waters of the Firth and which are guarded by the Souters of Cromarty. In view of the strategic location of the Cromarty Firth and its natural supplies of essential raw materials, it may be that it should be closely examined as the possible location of *Trucculensis Portus*.

References

Breeze, A. 'Philology on Tacitus's Graupian Hill and Trucculan Harbour' in *PSAS* Vol. 132. 2002

Gillen, C. 'The Physical Background' in *The Ross & Cromarty Book*, ed. Omand, D., Golspie. 1984

Hind, J. G. F. 'Agricola's Fleet and Portus Trucculensis' in *Britannia* Vol. v. 1974

Horsley, J. *Britannia Romana*, London, 1733 & Newcastle, 1974

Jones, G. D. B. & Mattingly, D. *An Atlas of Roman Britain*, Oxford. 1990

Keay J. & Keay, J. *Collins Encyclopaedia of Scotland*, London. 1994

MacKie, E. *Lecture given to SAS*, St. Andrews. 2000

Maclennan, A. 'Plant Life' in *The Ross and Cromarty Book*, ed. Omand. 1984

Martin, C. 'Water Transport and the Roman Occupations of North Britain' in *Scotland and the Sea*, ed. Smout, T. C., Edinburgh. 1992

Mason, D. J. P. *Roman Britain and the Roman Navy*, Stroud. 2003

Morrison, J. S. & Coates, J. F. *The Athenian Tireme: The history and reconstruction of an ancient Greek warship*, Cambridge. 1986

Reed, N. 'The Fifth Year of Agricola's Campaigns' in *Britannia* Vol. ii. 1971

Rivet, A. L. F. & Smith, C. *The Place-Names of Roman Britain*, London. 1979

Ross, S. M. *Personal Communication*. 2003

Spaul, J. *Classes Imperii Romani*, Nectoreca, Andover. 2002

Starr, C. G. *Roman Imperial Navy 31BC - AD324 3rd edition*, Ares Publishers. 1993

Steven, H. M. & Carlisle, A. *The Native Pinewoods of Scotland*. 1959

Taciti, C. *De Vita Agricolae*, ed. Ogilvie & Richmond, Oxford. 1967

Wolfson, S. *http://myweb.tiscali.co.uk/fartherlands/appendix.htm*

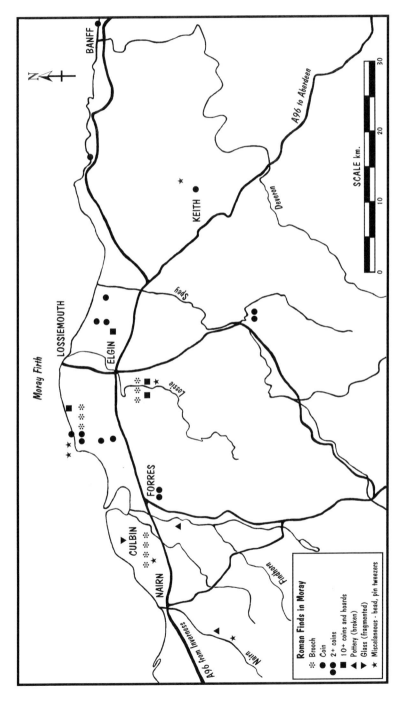

Figure 11: Location of Roman Finds in Moray

CHAPTER VI
Random Roman Finds in Moray

During the four hundred years of the Roman occupation of Britain, Moray was occasionally visited by Roman troops, but the scatter of Roman coins and artefacts, which have survived to be discovered during the last 150 years, indicates that there was periodical, though not necessarily continuous contact between native and Roman. Moray was a typical frontier area, different in location but no different in its treatment by the Romans to the vast lands of Eastern Europe and Western Asia which stretched beyond the Roman *limes* and which have produced such a wealth of material from graves and hoards. Where there is a difference is in the quantity of grave goods. This is a consequence of the paucity of Iron Age graves in Scotland, which may reflect differences in funeral practices or the destructive acidity of most of the Scottish soil.

It was Edward Luttwak (1976) who in his seminal work *The Grand Strategy of the Roman Empire* signalled the change from looking at the Roman frontier as a fixed boundary, with walls and guard posts, to a more fluid system, where bribery and corruption were used to control the tribes, though always with the threat of the legions if the Roman clients stepped too far out of line. This reappraisal of the frontier system was further developed by Jones (1978) when he emphasised the constraints that modern minds have in understanding the Roman concept of warfare. Today's inhabitants of the Middle East understand this concept all too well, but the continuation of fighting, after the battle has been lost, is an idea alien to the western mind. A concomitant of such a system of governance is utter ruthlessness by the occupying power, and in this the Romans were more than competent.

The two Birnie hoards are examples of Roman bribery and are described under the chapter entitled Birnie, but the Culbin sands have also proved to be a rich source of Roman material and this would indicate that much of the putative trade was maritime. The Culbin sands, now stabilised by tree planting, stretch between the rivers Nairn and Findhorn in the North-East of Scotland. There are few natural harbours on this north-facing coast, but the extensive sandy beaches of the Culbin were eminently suitable for sailing craft to move inshore at high tide, and as the water ebbed the boats settled safely on to the soft sand and could then be unloaded. Black (1891:484-511) wrote up an exhaustive examination of the objects found in the Culbin. Unfortunately he was not always too specific with a vague description of 'a considerable number of brooches' and it was left to the later activities of Curle (1932:391) and Henig (1971:231-3) to positively identify four of the brooches as Roman. One of these brooches, a magnificent gold crossbow type, now in the British Museum, is shown in Plate No. 15 of de la Bédoyère's volume of *The Finds of Roman Britain*. In 1966 the late R. B. K. Stevenson commented: 'the distant scattering of the brooches represents a move northwards ahead of the Roman army,' but with regard to the Culbin it may also indicate the movement of the Roman fleet, either mercantile or navy. A recent study by Hunter (2002: 43-50) makes a cogent argument for north Scotland and Ireland to be considered, not as isolated instances of recipients of Roman trade and the occasional mailed fist, but as part of a continuum of a frontier community stretching from the steppes of Russia to the shores of the Atlantic. The answers to the difficult questions concerning the disposition of Roman forces in Scotland may well be found in eastern Europe or even the Middle East.

Description	Grid Ref.	Finder or Reporter	Find Year
Enamelled Bronze Bird	NJ210 585	Hunter, F. *Excavs. at Birnie*, 2002 p17	2002
Brooch, copper & enamel	NJ210 585	Hunter, F. *Excavs. at Birnie*, 2001 p20	2001
Denarius 44 BC	NJ035 588	Bateson & Holmes PSAS 2003 p249	2000
Plate Brooch, 2nd-3rd cent.AD	NJ210 585	Hunter, F. *Excavs. at Birnie*, 1999 p16	1999
Trumpet Brooch 1st-2nd cent.	NJ210 585	Hunter, F. *Excavs. at Birnie*, 1999 p16	1999
Sestertius, Vespasian 1st cent	NJ290 640	Bateson & Holmes *PSAS* 2003 p249	1998
Denarius, Titus/Vesp. 80/81	NJ285 669	Bateson & Holmes *PSAS* 2003 p249	1997
Coin, Roman Bronze 3rd cent	NJ125 639	Bateson & Holmes *PSAS* 2003 p248	1997
Coin, Roman Bronze c.305	NJ236 710	Keillar, I. *Dis.& Exc. Scot.* 1990 p21	1990
Samian, type 31, 2nd AD	NH859 512	Pelling, R. *Man. Arch. Bull.* Vol. 5 p18	1990
Biconical blue bead	NH838 476	Gregory, R. *PSAS* Vol. 131 p197	1988
Coin, Roman unidentified	NJ035 590	Keillar, I. *Dis. & Exc. Scot.* 1984 p13	1984
14 coins, wcrn Bronze c.350	NJ176 708	Sekulla, M. Letter to I.A.G.S. 21.04.82	1979
Coin, Roman Bronze c.282	NJ135 693	Robertson, A. *PSAS* Vol.113 p414	1976
Coin, Roman Bronze c.351	NJ119 687	Robertson, A. *PSAS* Vol.113 p414	1976
Coin, antonin, Gallienusc c.260	NJ111 691	Keillar, I. *Dis.& Exc. Scot.* 1972 p15	1972
Gate pivot stone, Muiryfold	NJ489 522	Keillar, I. *Dis.& Exc. Scot.* 1972 p14	1972
Trumpet Brooch 2nd AD	NJ00 63	Henig, M. *PSAS* Vol.103 p231-2	1971
Silver signet ring 2nd AD	NJ00 63	Henig, M. *PSAS* Vol.103 p231-2	1971
Zoomorphic support 37mm	NJ00 63	Henig, M. *PSAS* Vol.103 p231-2	1971

Description	Grid Ref.	Finder or Reporter	Find Year
Coin, Greek Bronze, Nero	NJ110 690	Robertson, A. *PSAS* Vol.103 p161	1971
Bronze, Constans II. Banff	NJ685 645	Robertson, A. *PSAS* Vol.103 p157	1971
Bronze, Claudius II. Cullen	NJ514 672	Robertson, A. *PSAS* Vol.103 p157	1971
Bronze, Aurelian. Keith	NJ430 505	Robertson, A. *PSAS* Vol.103 p157	1971
4 Bronze 3rd-4th AD. Mortlach	NJ323 395	Robertson, A. *PSAS* Vol.103 p157	1971
4 Roman Bronze coins. Elgin	NJ220 630	Robertson, A. *PSAS* Vol.103 p161	1971
3 Roman Bronze coins. Forres	NJ035 590	Robertson, A. *PSAS* Vol.103 p161	1971
2 Brooches, pins, needles etc.	NJ 175 707	Robertson (ref. Curle) *Britannia* Vol. 1	1970
Coin, sestertius, J. Mamaea c.230	NJ223 613	Robertson, A. *PSAS* Vol. 103 p126	1968
Tessara, Roman c.1st-2nd AD	NJ324 571	Wood, K. (found in Lossie. Verified by BM)	1964
Roman glass, fragments	NJ00 63	Curle, J. from Culbin *PSAS* Vol. 66 p391	1932
3 Roman Brooches, 2nd AD	NJ00 63	Curle, J. from Culbin *PSAS* Vol. 66 p391	1932
171 coins, worn Bronze c.305	NJ176 708	Benton, S. *PSAS* Vol. 65 pp209-216	1930
Pottery, Roman, unidentified	NJ 005 498	Lauder, T. D. *NSA* Edenkillie p185	1842
Coin, denarius, Titus c.75AD	NJ047 595	Douglas, R. *Annals of Forres* p20	1843
Coins, Roman unidentified	NJ035 588	Douglas, R. *Annals of Forres* p20	1797

References

Black, G. F. 'Report on the Archaeological examination of the Culbin sands, Elginshire' in *PSAS* Vol. 25. 1891

Bédoyère, G. de la *The Finds of Roman Britain*, London. 1989

Curle, J. 'Culbin' in *PSAS* Vol. lxvi. 1932

Henig, J. 'Three Roman Objects from the Culbin Sands, Morayshire' in *PSAS* Vol. 103. 1971

Hunter, F. 'Problems in the Study of Roman and Native' in *Limes* Vol. xviii, *Jordan 2000*, Oxford. 2002

Jones, G. D. B. *Concept and Development in Roman Frontiers*, Manchester. 1978

Luttwak, E. *The Grand Strategy of the Roman Empire*, Baltimore. 1976

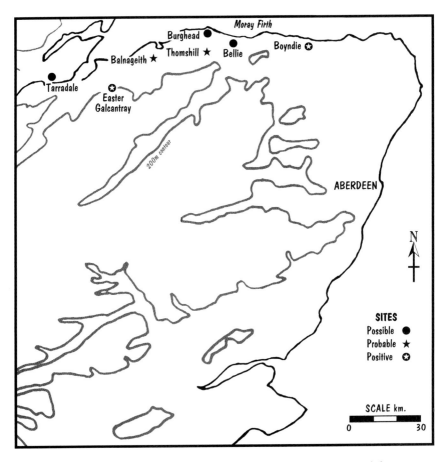

Figure 12: Roman Sites in Moray: Possible to Positive

CHAPTER VII
Possible Sites

As beauty is in the eye of the beholder so the definition of a possible Roman site is in the judgement of the categoriser. When does possibility shade into probability and probability become positive? The decision, any decision, is subjective. There is no such thing as an unbiased judgement. The following sites have mostly been excavated by the late Professor G. D. Barri Jones of Manchester University *[Figure 12]*. For fifteen years he came up to Moray practically every summer and engaged in both aerial reconnaissance and excavation. His flying was supported by the Moray Aerial Survey, an ad hoc group of enthusiasts who financed his operations, while the excavations were primarily supported by Manchester University with additional help from Newcastle University under Charles Daniels who worked for several seasons at Thomshill near Birnie. Sadly, Barri died in 1999, on the eve of an extended aerial survey, while Charles had died a few years earlier. Due to the unexpectedness of both deaths, their papers were left in some disorder, but it is satisfying to know that most of Barri's Scottish aerial photographs have been lodged with the RCAHMS who will shortly be producing a catalogue of them.

Bellie NJ358 618

The site, never closely examined by Jones, is on the first terrace above the east side of the Spey at 23 metres OD and adjacent to the B9104 Spey Bay road and some three kilometres from the sea. In the neighbourhood there are several cairns and a cist was found in 1868 adjacent to the supposed boundary of the camp. The site was mentioned in Macfarlane's *Geographical Collections*, published in 1726, while the ditches and earthworks are shown on estate maps dated some fifty years later. The adjoining cottage has the suggestive name of 'Roman Camp Gate', while the site has been commonly referred to, without much evidence, as *Tuesis*. During World War II the camp was used as a domestic site for the RAF adjacent airfield at Dallachy. Concrete bases were laid as the foundations for huts and washhouses and twenty years after the place was abandoned there was nothing but concrete and bare gravel visible. Careful examination recovered nothing which could indicate what the site had been used for in the recent past. Not a brass button nor a piece of broken mug was found. Later, Norwegian spruce trees were planted and these gave way to houses, and any chance of determining whether there was ever a Roman site there have now disappeared.

Almost forty years ago, Keillar and Skelton (1967) carried out a resistivity survey in an attempt to discover the south ditch but in this they were unsuccessful. Twenty years later, J. K. St. Joseph tried twice to find the line of the east ditch and was equally unsuccessful. Crawford (1949:122-4) discusses the site very well and points out that it was first mentioned in Macfarlane's *Geographical Collections* in 1726. Crawford was himself all prepared to carry out an archaeological excavation of the site when the outbreak of war prevented the work being carried out, but, as he wryly comments, 'The war has also made future investigations much more difficult for the camp-site has now reverted to its presumed original purpose.' The size is, or rather was, 400ft x 900ft, giving an area of 8.25 acres. Crawford concludes his comments: 'there is still an element of uncertainty that only excavation can clear up.'

Long subsequent to Crawford's comments and immediately to the south-west of the site, Barclay (1993:255-68) in 1990 excavated an iron age settlement which revealed some Mesolithic flints, no pottery, and a few grains of barley. However, carbon dating indicates that this native site has no relevance to its alleged Roman neighbour. Further to the south-west, in the vicinity of Bellie graveyard, are three distinct circular crop marks and a straight cropmark leading into a wide circular corner. Excavation by the late C. M. Daniels showed that the crop mark was caused by a fine red sandstone pavement or perhaps foundation for a turf wall. Adjacent to the castle there are many crop-marks, but enthusiasm has to be tempered by the realisation that during Medieval and into modern times there were deer parks, gardens and military establishments associated with Gordon Castle; all of which have left their crop-marks for posterity to puzzle over.

If ever a site deserves the old Scottish verdict of 'not proven' it is Bellie. It is the natural rendezvous for the army to meet up with the Agricolan fleet. Yet, Crawford was cautious and the indefatigable J. K. St. Joseph could uncover no evidence so, on balance, it cannot even scrape into the 'probable' category and must remain classified as 'possible'.

Burghead NJ111 691

The Torfness, maybe, of the Sagas, is unlikely, despite its 'Roman' well, to have been built by the legions. Roy's fine engraving (Roy 1793:Pl.xxxiii), which displays Burghead before the improvers got to work, shows no hint of Roman regularity. Devotees of a Roman presence explain away any irregularities in construction as due to the builders being marines and not legionary craftsmen. Maybe so, but the marines must also have had access to the fleet wine ration. The 19th century antiquarians had no reservations. Burghead was a Roman station and the famous well, now classed as a Christian baptistery, was firmly categorised as 'Roman'. However, recent carbon-14 dates and those from Alan Small's excavation from the sixties give dates subsequent to the Roman period.

The well was uncovered in 1809 and not long after was deepened by gunpowder in an attempt to increase the water flow. This was unsuccessful and must raise the question as to whether it ever was originally intended as a source of water or a bath. There is no facility to remove any overflow and the water supply has always depended upon seepage and not from some firm subterranean source. Firth (2004) makes the intriguing but somewhat unlikely suggestion that the well building should be examined to see if it possibly could be a temple to Mithras. Mithras was a deity popular amongst soldiers of the Roman Empire and reached his height of popularity in the 3rd century AD.

Roy (1793:131-2) was quite firm in his opinion: 'It may be proper to remark that this place is undoubtedly the Ptoroton and Alata Castra of Ptolemy.' However, Robert Young (1868:3) makes the comment 'If the Romans occupied Burghead, the period of occupation, perhaps, was not long.' Robert Young's son, Hugh (1899:5-17), a competent antiquarian, gave a paper at Inverness on 30th June 1899 at which he presented the evidence for Roman occupation at Burghead and concluded: 'The blue melon bead and bone pin found in the lower fort have been pronounced by the British Museum authorities to be undoubtedly Roman. The axe and ballista stone have also been pronounced to be Roman by the only good authority to whom I have had an opportunity of showing them.'

Mrs Grant (1950:78) of Rothiemurchus, an intelligent and well educated woman, writes: '...a gentleman and his sister, who showed us coins, vases, and spear-heads found on excavating for some purpose in their close neighbourhood at Burghead, all Roman; on going lower the workmen came upon a bath, a spring enclosed by stone cut walls, a mosaic pavement surrounding the bath, steps descending to it, and paintings on the walls. The place was known to have been a Roman station with many others along the south side of the Moray Firth.'

Gregory (2001a:215) makes the comment 'Indeed, the occupation of Burghead during the Roman period does seem possible due to the recovery of a melon bead from the site.' Alas, beads and Roman coins, which have also been uncovered at Burghead, are eminently portable and therefore, not conclusive evidence. However, they are sufficient, taking into account other evidence such as ballista balls etc. that Burghead should rate as a possibility. Perhaps the last word should lie with the local historian, Jeffrey (1928:6): 'Altogether, the arguments for and against the Roman origin of the fortifications appear to be pretty well balanced; so... the question may be fairly said to be still an open one.' In the last eighty years the balance has tipped further away from Burghead being a Roman station and the most optimistic classification is that of a doubtful 'possible.'

Tarradale NH545 490

Tucked away at the head of the Beauly Firth and some 500m north-west of Tarradale House is a complex of crop marks which, while inadequately examined, due to no fault of the excavators, indicates habitation or use from the Mesolithic to the medieval. Gregory (2001b:241-266) has done a sterling service in writing up the site, following upon the sudden and tragic death of Professor G. D. Barri Jones. Only a small part of the extensive site could be examined and even this was eventually curtailed due to difficulties with the agricultural regime.

The major part of the site examined was enclosed within the curve of a crop mark on a saddle of sandy soil at the northernmost boundary of the site [Plate 1]. Immediately outside the curve of the ditch there were several pits in which were discovered three bent hand-made nails. Whether these were nails used to hold up lattice work to stabilise the ditch or an attempt at making *lilia* has not been determined. If *lilia*, the question must be asked as to what were the nails used for?

Inside the curve of the enclosing ditch, a hearth, associated with pottery sherds, was uncovered while some burnt timber provided carbon-14 dates. The pottery appears to be from the Pictish period while two of the carbon-14 measurements give dates between 5,000 and 5,500BC, while the third is about 750BC. Without further long and careful excavation it is not possible to reach any conclusion on the site. It is badly eroded and it is very complicated and, despite its good strategic position is unlikely to have been used by the Romans.

References

Barclay, G. J. 'The excavation of pit circles at Romancamp Gate, Fochabers, Moray 1990' in *PSAS* Vol. 123. 1993

Crawford, O. G. S. *Topography of Roman Scotland,* Cambridge. 1949

Firth, H. N. *personal communication.* 2004

Grant, E. *Memoirs of a Highland Lady,* London. 1950

Gregory, R. A. 'Excavations by the late G. D. B. Jones and C. M. Daniels along the Moray Firth littoral' in *PSAS* Vol. 131. 2001a

Gregory, R. A. 'Survey and excavation at Tarradale, Highland' in *PSAS* Vol. 131. 2001b

Jeffrey, A. *Sketches from the Traditional History of Burghead,* Aberdeen. 1928

Roy, W. *The Military Antiquities of the Romans in North Britain,* London. 1793

Young, H. W. 'Burghead' in *Trans. North. Ass. Lit. & Scien. Socs.* Vol. ii, Part vi. 1899

Young, R. *Notes on Burghead: Ancient and Modern,* Elgin. 1868

CHAPTER VIII
Probable Sites

Just as the designation of a site as 'possible', with all the ambiguity which this implies, so the decision to designate a site as 'probable' is equally subjective, except that there is a greater degree of probability that a site is Roman than if it had been labelled 'possible'. Students of semantics may wish to discuss the precise weight of evidence at which 'possible' becomes 'probable', but the answer must lie in the individual mind, and since all minds are different, the criteria for determining the change becomes personal.

Thomshill: Birnie NJ210 573

The site is on an eroded spur which sits behind the village of Thomshill adjacent to a drainage channel which, in former times, diverted all or part of the Lossie's water from a point near the farm of Upper Bogside down to Waukmill at the east end of Elgin. The site overlooks the one-time farm of The Foths. George Gordon (1835:86), the polymathic minister of the parish, wrote: 'The remaining antiquities comprehend ...rectangular trenches, or as some say, a Roman castra at the Foths.' The soil is particularly light and is subject to severe aeolian erosion in a windy spring. By 1980 the rectangular trenches had been reduced to a barely visible L-shaped crop-mark, which subsequent aerial photography increased to a three-sided rectilinear enclosure *[Figure 13]*.

Between 1985 and 1990 the late C. M. Daniels of Newcastle University cut a number of sections across the ditches. The ditches were generally of V-shaped profile with clear and distinct shovel slots. 'The ditches were cut through sand, though there was some gravel, and the bottom slot and part of the profile was filled with small stones and silt' (Daniels et al 1985:8). Within the crop-mark was a mound which,

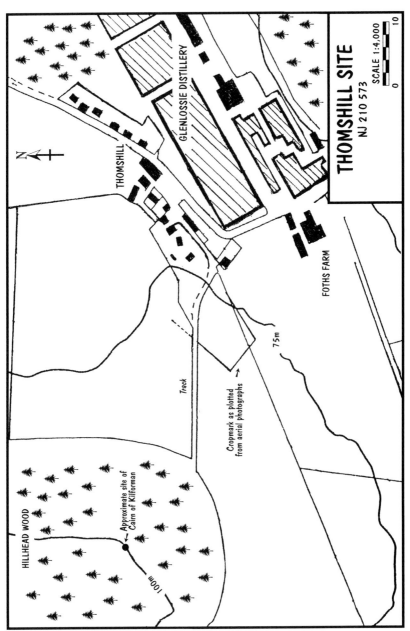

Figure 13: Thomshill

when investigated, contained ashes and household rubbish dating to the 1950's and which had its genesis in wind-blown sand which had formed a mini-dune at some time in the historical past. Gregory (2001: 177-222) gives a comprehensive description of C. M. Daniels's excavations. Although there were no useful findings, aeolian erosion having removed about one metre of surface soil and sand, the shape of the enclosure and the ditches is strongly suggestive of Roman work. It is too small for a marching camp, but at 4.3 acres (1.75 hectares) could have housed a quingenary, a five-hundred-strong auxiliary unit. At a distance of 1 km from Thomshill is the undefended Iron Age site of Birnie and it is tempting to associate the two sites as being mutually advantageous to each other. The Romans supplied protection and in return were able to obtain food and home comforts from the natives. However, there is no evidence of this, and as nothing specifically Roman has been found at Thomshill, it must be reluctantly consigned to the category of 'probable'.

Balnageith NJ025 578

is located on an abandoned World War II airfield on the flood plain of the Findhorn. The author had been looking for years across this plain for a Roman camp and it was not until July 1989 that Jones and Keillar (1990) incurred the wrath of a householder by venturing closer in an aircraft to the residential area of Forres and thus discovering the initial two straight crop-marks joined by a fine curve *[Plate 2]*. Coincidentally, like Thomshill and Birnie, the site is one km from an apparent native settlement which lies adjacent to the A96, Aberdeen to Inverness road.

Excavations commenced in September 1989 and the first trench, through the shorter arm of the crop-mark, exposed a V-shaped ditch some 2.7m across with a depth beneath the existing top soil of 1.2m. Another trench across the corner was again V-shaped with a sump which, photographs show, is clearly revetted (Keillar 1999) *[Plate 3]*. Behind the corner was found several shallow possible post holes which might represent the truncated evidence for a corner tower, but the evidence is far from conclusive and has not been used in any evaluation of the evidence.

Ground-penetrating radar indicated the extent of the longer arm of the crop mark and suggested the possibility of a *titulum*. The estimated size of the site is 6 acres (2.4 hectares) and this could hold about 1,000 men. Being adjacent to a river with an estuary it could have been a fleet depot as well as an army base. However, with no surviving finds and no carbon-14 dates this promising site must be categorised as 'probable'.

References

Daniels, C. M., Jones, G.D.B., Keillar, I. *In Fines Borestorum,* unpublished manuscript. 1985

Gordon, G. '1835 Parish of Birnie' in *NSA,* Edinburgh. 1845

Gregory, R. A. 'Excavations by the late G. D. B. Jones and C. M. Daniels along the Moray Firth Littoral' in *PSAS* Vol. 131. 2001

Jones, G. D. B. & Keillar, I. *Balnageith, Forres (Grampian Region),* privately circulated. 1990

Keillar, I. 'Obituary: Barri Jones: Professor of Archaeology' in *Bull. Moray Field Club* Vol. 27. 1999

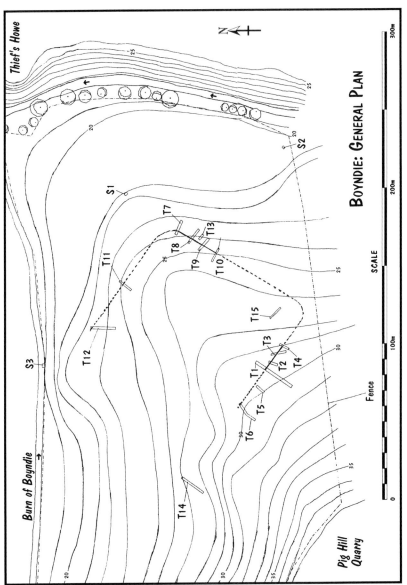

Figure 14: Boyndie

Chapter IX
Positive Sites

There are two positive Roman sites in greater Moray. These are sites which are definitely Roman beyond reasonable doubt and the implications of accepting this reality should be accepted and further explored. The Roman invasions of north Scotland are not simple to understand and it may be that the importance of the Roman navy has been underestimated. The number and extent of military invasions is imperfectly understood and it may be that Agricola was not the first general to advance into the north and his victory at Mons Graupius may not be as great as his son-in-law would have us believe. To those who do not wish to believe that the Romans advanced into Moray; there must be an explanation for those large rectangular sites, so different in scale and shape to the native products. Who dug these V shaped ditches, many with shovel slots or sumps? This may be a defensive argument but is still worthy of an answer. As Tercullian said '*certum est quia impossible*' – 'It must be true because it is impossible.' Only, in the case of the Romans in Moray, it is eminently possible.

Boyndie NJ654 636
is a difficult and most unlikely site and one which was discovered by accident. On Thursday 6th July 1989, Ian Keillar was driving Barri Jones along the A98 road towards Banff when approaching the B9121 the driver saw what appeared to be crop-marks on the sloping ground rising to the Hills of Boyndie. The crop was oil seed rape and despite in subsequent years, different crops have been grown, there has never been the slightest evidence of any subsequent crop-mark. The crop-mark appeared once, and once only. Ground radar was used in September 1989 to establish the location of the ditches and trial trenching of the site commenced in September 1990. Some fourteen trenches were

opened on the three sides which were reasonably delimited by the crop-marks *[Figure14]* (Jones 1991:226). Every trench was severely degraded and very difficult to analyse. There was evidence that aeolian action had reduced the surface by over one metre but it was not possible to establish in what sort of time scale this had occurred. One small shard of abraded Roman pottery was uncovered from an unstratified layer on the site, but this has been subsequently lost. Gregory (2001:210) gives the dimensions as 120m x 110m, thus enclosing an area of 3.1 acres (1.3 hectares). The evidence for this being a Roman site is very slight, except for one compelling piece of evidence which has now been lost.

On the same evening as that of the discovery, Barri Jones flew from Dalcross and carried with him a video recorder. As the aircraft flew round the site the recording showed the somewhat indistinct crop-marks until, at one position on the circuit, the image suddenly developed into the 3D appearance of a Roman fort, complete with corner turrets. This image lasted but a second and, as the aircraft completed the circuit there was nothing to see but the usual indistinct marks. This video was shown to various interested and knowledgeable people and in each case the response was the same: 'That is a Roman fort.' Alas, the tape has been lost and the opportunity to examine this unique evidence has gone. But that fleeting second of evidence is enough to move Boyndie from 'possible' to 'positive'.

So what was its purpose? Looking at the topography now it is very difficult to imagine any particular reason for its location. However, it is possible to visualise a time when the Burn of Boyndie was broader than it is now, and unfettered by the drifting sand which now impedes its progress, it discharged into an estuary between Whitehills and Banff. Ships could then move upstream into the sheltered waters fronting the fort. Anderson (1842:225), writing in the NSA, states: 'not far from the site of the old mansion house of Buchragie, may be traced the huge remains of what possibly have been a Roman camp.' According to Blaeu (1654), Buchragie lay on the west side of the Boyndie at NJ659 644, approximately where the B9139 road intersects with the B9038, while the earthwork was at NJ659 645. Diligent field-walking has failed to discover any such camp, but, in accordance with Roman examples elsewhere, where a marching camp is adjacent to a fort, it still remains a possibility. However, what is not possible, but is absolutely positive, is the fort site at Boyndie.

Easter Galcantry (Cawdor) NJ807 483

This is a complicated multi-period site situated beside the river Nairn which has removed some two-thirds of the original structure. It was first photographed by the Royal Commission in 1979 and again by Jones in 1984 who was immediately attracted by the fine straight crop-mark with a clear gateway located in the middle *[Plate 4]*. Whatever its earlier associations it was definitely an early modern graveyard as the then farmer, Mr. Davidson, now deceased, recollected removing tall undecorated grave-stones from the field and tipping them into the Nairn (Keillar 1999:35). The other end of the time scale is represented by a carbon-14 date of about 3,700BC, during the early Neolithic.

The ditch, particularly where excavated on the west side is characteristically diagnostic. It is distinctly V-shaped and when first exposed had a neat row of stones laid along the bottom. The excavators removed these stones and, unfortunately, most photographs do not show this distinctive feature. Within the site there were post holes associated with interior buildings and amongst those a blue glass pierced biconical bead was discovered (Jones 1988:425). This was erroneously described by Jones & Keillar (2002:8) as a blue melon bead; however, both types of bead are characteristic of the Iron Age extending to the Viking and indicate approximately when the site was occupied. A more accurate indication is given by a carbon-14 sample taken from a carbon layer taken from trench No. 2 which cut the west ditch. This sample gives a date of AD80-120.

This ditch showed clear indications of having been recut *[Plate 5]*, and also evidence that it had been manually refilled. A shard of Medieval

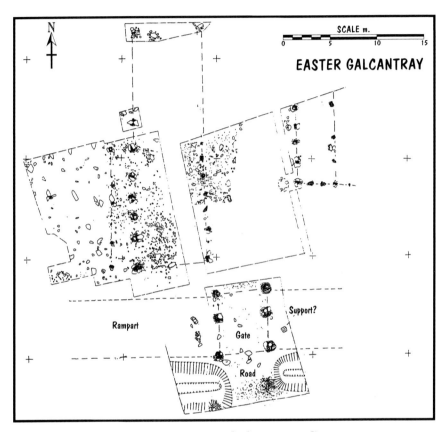

Figure 15: Easter Galcantray: Gate

pottery, circa AD1300, was also uncovered from the site. The entrance was 4.5m wide and behind it were 6 large post holes, ranging in diameter from in excess of half a metre to over one metre. Judging by the size of timbers, the gate defensive structure must have been massive *[Figure 15]*.

The estimated enclosed original area amounted to 4.32 acres (1.75 hectares) and was probably designed to house an auxiliary quingenary unit of 500 men. In location, though not in size, Easter Galcantry is similar to the fortlet at Gatehouse of Fleet NX595 575 (Keppie 1986:89). However the latter is estimated to have held a century, ie. eighty men.

The reasons given for not accepting that Easter Galcantry is Roman are that it is univallate and the internal arrangements are not in accordance with accepted Roman practice. However, few first-century forts have survived and it can be argued that the legions who built the fort and presumably others in Moray were severely restricted for time and, after the allegedly decisive battle of Mons Graupius, had neither fear nor expectation of any uprising, and thus only dug a single ditch. The arguments for in being classed as 'positive' are the magnificent ditch sections, particularly the west with its neat row of sump stones. Then there is the fine gateway with its massive timbers and the carbon date which falls conveniently into the Flavian period. The balance tips on to the positive side and, by so doing, incrementally increases the chances, though not decisively, that the sites labelled 'probable' may well be 'positive' and the possible could then move up the probability ladder to 'probable'.

So, from the long known site at Bellie to the site at Boyndie, whose veracity is purely subjective, there are seven sites in greater Moray which, at some time, may have been considered as Roman. Only two have survived examination and are considered 'positive' but that docs not exclude the possibility that future research will discover new sites.

References

Anderson, A. '1842 The Parish of Boindie' in *NSA*, Edinburgh. 1845

Blaeu, J. *Aberdonia & Banfia*, Amsterdam. 1654

Gregory, R. A. 'Excavations by the late G. D. B. Jones and C. M. Daniels along the Moray Firth Littoral' in *PSAS* Vol. 131. 2001

Jones, G. D. B. 'Cawdor' in *Britannia* Vol. xix. 1988

Jones, G. D. B. 'Boyndie' in *Britannia* Vol. xxii. 1991

Jones, G. D. B. & Keillar, I. 'Archaeological Landscapes of Moray' in *Northern Scotland* Vol. 22. 2002

Keillar, I. 'The Romans in Moray' in *Moray Field Club Bulletin*. Vol. 27. 1999

Keppie, L. *Scotland's Roman Remains*, Edinburgh. 1986

CHAPTER **X**
Birnie: The Two Hoards

Archaeological Excavations at Dykeside of Birnie

Following his successful completion of the excavation of the Deskford Carnyx site, Hunter (1999) started investigation of a site (NJ210 585), originally discovered by Jones et al (1993:47-74). The site had been marked out for investigation since 1996 when a Mr Hamish Stuart had discovered 18 Roman silver coins on the site when using a metal detector. The site lies on a sand and gravel terrace sloping down to the north and sheltered by higher ground to the south and west. The original aerial photographs showed a number of what were believed, and turned out, to be hut circles.

Field walking revealed some casual use of the site in the Neolithic and Bronze Ages with evidence from broken pottery of a Medieval presence, while slag and clinker indicated metal working, also of a presumed Medieval age. By the year 2000, several more coins had been discovered while two Roman brooches had been found (Hunter 2000:16) - one a trumpet brooch made somewhere in Britain and the other an enamelled plate brooch which had its origins in 2nd or early 3rd century north-west Europe.

But the year 2000 was Millennium year and, coming in with a bang, was to go out with a bang, at least as far as Dykeside of Birnie was concerned. A season of field work, involving finding and plotting the location of every stray coin led, inevitably, to the discovery of a hoard of some 300 Roman denarii, originally contained in a leather pouch once placed inside a native pot which had been lined with bracken *[Plates 6 & 7]*. At the time of writing his report, Hunter (2001:15) noted that the number of coins now numbered 313 and ranged in age from Nero to

Severus, with the latest coin being minted in AD196-7. All were *denarii* with silver content lowering steadily from Nero through to Severus and his vicious son, Caracalla, who reduced the silver percentage to only 40%.

But if the year 2000 was *annus millennium* then 2001 must be *annus mirabilis*, for Hunter and his team uncovered another hoard of Roman coins just 10m away from the first (Hunter 2002:18) *[Plate 8]*. A preliminary and cursory examination showed that the coins were *denarii*, similar to the first hoard, surrounded by vegetation, and put in a pot of apparent native manufacture. The coinage was slightly earlier in date than the first hoard, the latest coin being minted in 193AD. A fine Roman brooch, made of copper alloy and decorated with enamel and silver was also found elsewhere, while an Edwardian (Plantagenet) silver penny helped to confirm the Medieval status of part of the site.

It was far too much to expect the discovery of a third hoard and indeed this would have been most unlikely as, after the discovery of the second hoard, the whole area had been examined by very sensitive commercial metal detecting equipment. But slow, methodical excavation is continuing to tease out the nature of the location of the coin hoard find-spot while differentiating between the Iron Age and Medieval remains.

The fine Roman brooches indicate that the site was of high status during the late Iron Age but it has not yet been determined whether there was any link, during the Medieval period, with the adjacent religious site of Birnie.

Birnie and the Early Bishopric of Moray
The old kirk at Birnie *[Plate 9]* has long been recognised as the site of the first bishopric of Moray. The date of the establishment of the bishopric is not definite. According to Donaldson and Morpeth (1977:154) the first bishop was Gregory, circa 1114, and was subject directly to the Pope, until placed under the metropolitan authority of St. Andrews in 1472. Barrow (1989:1-16), in writing of the church in

Badenoch and Strathspey, does not name the first bishop of Moray and, as Duncan (1975:104) succinctly puts it: 'The foundation of bishop's sees, however, is also obscure.' Thus while the date of the foundation is not precisely known, it was very probably in the latter days of Alexander I (1107-1124).

According to the Moray Register (1837:xii) the first bishop was Gregory, followed by William, Felix 1162-1171, Simon de Toeni 1171-1189 and Richard 1187-1203. It is probable that there is an unknown bishop between Gregory and William and it may be that it was during this unknown bishops's reign that the existing Birnie kirk was constructed. Following Richard was Brice de Douglas who based himself at Kinneddar and early petitioned the Pope that the cathedral of Moray, which had perambulated between Birnie, Kinneddar and Spynie, be fixed at Spynie.

The existing kirk of Birnie, which incorporates most of the fabric of the first cathedral, is built on a low knoll and houses an early Celtic bell. The suggestion that Birnie is somehow cognate with St. Brendan is fanciful, as it can be easily demonstrated that there is a lineal line of succession from the early Gaelic meaning of a moist place to the modern name of Birnie. Sharing the knoll with the kirk is a Class I Pictish stone, while the whole appearance and indeed atmosphere of the place is indicative that here there was once a stone circle.

Stone circle or not, this was once a high-status site. Even in this secular age, Birnie is still 'special' in an ill-definable way. Is there any connection between the high-status site of Birnie kirk and the high-status site of Dykeside of Birnie? At present there is no relationship except their geographical proximity. Here are two sites, separated by 1,000 years of time and one kilometre of space. Hard-headed Romans thought that the inhabitants of Birnie were worthy of bribery, while a thousand years later the equally hard-headed prelates of the Roman church thought that Birnie was worthy of being honoured by the erection of the first cathedral of Moray. Is this coincidence or is there something special about Birnie?

The Coin Hoards

What we do know is special about Birnie is the discovery of two hoards of Roman coins buried within 10 metres of each other. Coin hoards are not unusual on the periphery of the Roman Empire, but what is unusual is that here there are two. Initial analysis (Hunter 2003:22-25) shows that there were 310 coins in the second hoard and 315 in the first, while the coins in the second hoard are of marginally younger dates than the first hoard. As Hunter points out, this suggests a repeated relationship with Rome.

Simplistically, we can assume that these hoards were bribes from Rome to a local chieftain to keep the peace. But why? Was it because there were Roman traders in the locality, or even detachments of Roman troops? If either one or the other, or even both, the question must be, what were they up to and where did they live? As we know from the Epitome of Dio Cassius (1986:109): 'The Caledonians did not remain true to their promises and had made preparations to assist the Maeatae, and since at the time Severus was embroiled in war elsewhere, Lupus (Governor in Britain) was forced to buy peace from the Maeatae for a large sum, and in exchange recovered a few captives.' But bribery and corruption were not unique to Scotland. All over northern and eastern Europe there are coin hoards which indicate that while, in the ultimate, the emperor was prepared to send in the legions, the preferred means of border control was by the payment of cash. Not that the recipients had a monetary economy, but coin was a convenient and easily dividable way of handling silver, while the actual presence of the two hoard indicates not only contact with but a relationship with Rome. We can only hypothesise as to its nature.

References

Barrow, G. W. S. 'Badenoch and Strathspey 2: The Church' in *Northern Scotland* Vol. 9, Aberdeen. 1989

Cassius, D. in *Roman Britain*, ed. Ireland, S., New York. 1986

Donaldson, G. & Morpeth, R. S. *A Dictionary of Scottish History*, Edinburgh. 1977

Duncan, A. A. M. *Scotland - The Making of the Kingdom*, Edinburgh. 1975

Hunter, F. *Fieldwork at Birnie, Moray, 1998*, NMS, Edinburgh, 1999

Hunter, F. *Fieldwork at Birnie, Moray, 1999*, NMS, Edinburgh, 2000

Hunter, F. *Fieldwork at Birnie, Moray, 2000*, NMS, Edinburgh, 2001

Hunter, F. *Fieldwork at Birnie, Moray, 2001*, NMS, Edinburgh, 2002

Hunter, F. *Fieldwork at Birnie, Moray, 2002*, NMS, Edinburgh, 2003

Jones, B., Keillar, I. & Maude, K. 'The Moray Aerial Survey: discovering the prehistoric and protohistoric landscape' in Sellar, W. D. H. *Moray, Province & People*, Edinburgh. 1993

REM = Cockburn, H. T. ed. *Registrum Episcoptus Moraviensis (Moray Register)*, Edinburgh. 1837

Chapter XI
Janus: Looking Backwards and Forwards

Janus was one of the oldest Latin gods. He was always represented as two-faced, or looking both ways, and thus gave his name to the first month of the year in the modern calendar, where one simultaneously looks back on the year that has gone and forward to the year that is coming. Oddly enough, the Romans dedicated the fifth month of their year to Janus. With his ability to look forward and back, Janus is ideally placed to complete this survey of Moray and remind us of what has been missed while looking forward to what may yet be found. The places mentioned below are listed neither alphabetically, chronologically, thematically, nor in order of significance. The theme perhaps is new and old approaches, with acknowledgement to Hunter (2001:289-309).

The Bridge of Spey NJ319 519

The Medieval bridge spanned the Spey just to the north of the existing railway bridge at Boat o' Brig. In the Moray Register (1837:123) is a charter issued in AD1235 to Muriel of Rothes referring to the hospital of St. Nicholas '*juxta pontem de Spey*'. In the dry summer of 1976 there was a broad, about 8m wide, linear parch mark visible on the haugh land lying to the east of Orton House (NJ314 539). It may be that this indicated the line of a road which once led to the bridge but the construction of the railway has effectively obliterated any traces nearer the river. Leslie (1795:90) noted that part of the foundation pier of the bridge still remained but presumably this was removed in the great flood of 1829, for according to Forbes (1834:365), 'This bridge... its erection has been ascribed to the Romans in their progress under Severus, and it is known to have been in existence after the Reformation.... Not a vestige of its ruins has been visible for many years.'

Forres NJ040 588

was once a Royal Burgh, but like all the other ancient burghs, hundreds of years of tradition and heritage were swept into the dustbin of history by the 1970's reformers. Forres was once thought to have been the *Boresti* of Tacitus but with no other evidence than imagination, this suggestion is no longer considered tenable. Robert Douglas (1934:20), medical officer of health and historian of Forres, writes:

> *In November, 1797, in the streets of Forres, there were dug up several Roman coins and a Roman medallion in soft metal which resembled a mixture of lead and tin.... A copper coin of the time of the Emperor Titus was found near Sweno's Stone in 1843, one side was an outline of the head of the Emperor encircled with bay. The profile looks to the left. Above the head is the inscription – 'Vespasianus Rom. Imp. Avg.' On the reverse side, on the right, is a female figure under the shade of a palm tree. Above there is 'Ivdaea Capta', and under are the letters 'S.C.' meaning 'Senatus Consultum.'*

> *On 25ᵗʰ September, 1844, another Roman coin was found in Forres of the reign of one of the Caesars... it is thought to have belonged to the reign of Domitian, AD81.... These finds in themselves are no evidence of Roman occupation. These coins may have been carried to Forres by others or may have been brought to Forres by the Romans themselves on trading visits to this district.*

At the east end of Forres, there is the Cluny Hill, on the summit of which there are the difficult-to-discern remains of a native fort. At the foot of the hill there are barely a couple of kilometres of flat land between the hill and the sea, and any invading army marching from the east would be constrained to pass through this narrow gap. Only the presence of Sueno's Stone indicates that at least on one occasion there was a decisive battle here.

The Cloves Head NJ139 612

Cloves is a farm, a kilometre and a half south of the village of Alves. In the mid-1860's a marble head, somewhat larger than full size, was discovered at a now unidentifiable location. The hair was in small tight curls and the opinion was that the head had belonged to a religious statue, probably removed from Pluscarden. The head was retained in the offices of the *Forres Gazette* and has long since disappeared. Rumour has it that perhaps the wife of Gordon-Cumming, of the baccarat scandal, took the head to Altyre, but a cursory examination of the gardens there has not disclosed anything.

Alleged Signal Station, Ben Rinnes NJ26 37

At a location, now lost, there was a circular depression, some few metres across, surrounded by a very low turf bank. From the site it was possible to see the mouth of the Spey, Burghead and the Souters of Cromarty. With the bulk of the hill behind the site, it was not possible for any signals to be read towards the interior of the country.

Aerial Magnetic Survey

Over thirty years ago, Rio Tinto Zinc, as it then was, carried out a series of aerial magnetic surveys in the North-East to determine the feasibility of mining metals such as copper etc. The results were encouraging, but the metal discovered, while extensive in volume was, as yet, too low grade to make mining economic. However, if the battle of Mons Graupius had taken place in the North-East then, subsequent to the victory, the Romans would presumably bury all the scrap metal that they did not wish to take away with them. This buried metal could produce a very intense magnetic anomaly.

An approach to Rio Tinto at their office in Bristol led to a very positive response and the supply of several magnetic survey charts. None showed any intense magnetic anomalies, but Rio Tinto has more charts, not then available, and a further approach might be useful.

Miscellaneous 1. Inverugie NK102 488

Surrounding the motte is a very faint, but discernible, rectangular crop-mark with rounded corners. Apparently there is a similar motte within a rectangular embankment in Wales at Tomen-y-mur.

Miscellaneous 2. Rosskeen NH680 693

Linear crop-mark running parallel to farm road from Rosskeen farm heading west. Fine curve near railway line and crop mark then continues approximately in northern direction.

Miscellaneous 3. Berridale ND115 228

Large rectangular crop-mark on plateau between castle site and Langwell House.

Keith and Surroundings NJ430 505

Keith and its environs have long been associated in popular mythology with battles and Romans. The Ballochs have been canvassed as the site of the battle of Mons Graupius. One hundred and fifty years before St. Joseph (1951:65) discovered the site at Auchinhove, Forbes (1791:555) was writing in the OSA 'Auchinhove, which lies near the banks of the Isla, has been another field of battle: and in a line with it, towards Cullen, upon the head of the burn of Altmore, some pieces of armour were said to have been dug up several years ago, but were not preserved'. At Muiryfold, site of a known Roman marching camp, a Roman lower pivot stone for gate was discovered over thirty years ago and is now in the Elgin museum. Authentication of the find was by the late Professor G. D. B. Jones who had found a similar artefact on a Roman gold-mining site in Spain.

Tuesis Polis

According to Müller (1883:89-95), *Tuesis aestuarium* has co-ordinates of 27° east and 59° north while *Tuesis polis* has co-ordinates of 26° 45′ east and 59° 10′ north. These figures are confirmed by Stevenson (1991:49-50) and indicate that if the *Tuesis* estuary is correctly positioned, than the settlement of the same name, being 10′ further north, must lie somewhere 15 kilometres off shore in the Moray Firth. Of course, Ptolemy might have got his co-ordinates transposed, in which case *Tuesis polis* lies some 15km up river from the mouth of the river. As mentioned earlier, *Tuesis* has long been accepted as the Spey, though Watson (1926:31) somewhat hesitantly states '*Tuesis* was probably on the river of that name, identified with Spey.' Jackson (1955:151) has no difficulty in equating *Tuesis* with the Spey while Rivet and Smith (1979:481) do likewise.

Tuesis Polis has been somewhat neglected by the authorities. Unlike *Pinnata castra* it has not been removed to Inchtuthill and it was not until the nineteen-nineties that a determined effort was made to establish its location, when Strang (1997:22, 1998:436), in a couple of seminal papers, which comprehensively reassess Ptolemy and his work in Britain, places the *polis* either near Rothes or Aberlour. The essence of Strang's analysis is contained in his 1997 paper when he writes: 'Ptolemy's map of Britain embraces two distinct longitudinal, angular scales, that for England (41.67 Rm. *[= Roman miles]* per degree) being substantially greater than for Scotland/Ireland (25.8 Rm. per degree). Although the latitudinal scale is common for Britain as a whole (62.5 Rm. per degree), and that it is misleading to apply a linear scale (eg. Rm per cm) to a substantially distorted map.'

Using distances and directions from known Roman sites such as Colchester and York and applying localised corrections to areas surrounding established sites such as Trimontium etc., Strang has been able to correct Ptolemy's map and establish, with much greater accuracy then hitherto, the location of as yet unlocated Roman sites. Quoting Strang (1997:22), '*Tuesis* should be located on the *Tuesis Fl.* (R. Spey), possibly at Newlands near Rothes.' '*Pinnata Castra* locates just to the east of Burghead.'

Following his 1997 paper, Strang (1998:436) revised his location of *Tuesis polis* from being near Rothes to the vicinity of Aberlour. This is probably not a reasonable location. The Spey is a fast-flowing river.

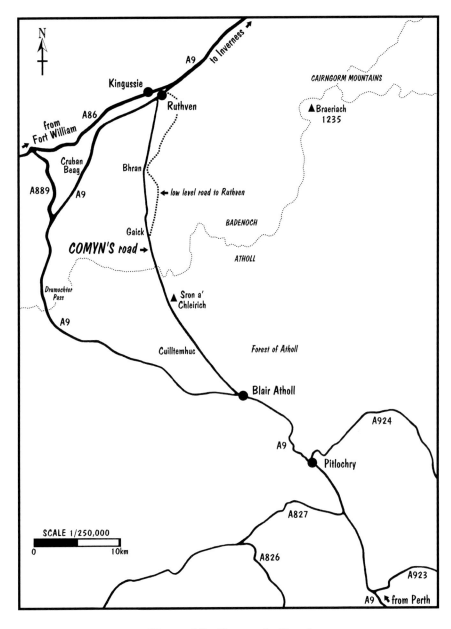

Figure 16: Comyn's Road

According to Barr (2004), it has an average velocity of 13 miles per hour; a speed far in excess of that capable from either an oar or sail propelled vessel. Accordingly, if *Tuesis polis* was near Aberlour then any Roman supply ships would have had to be towed up stream for some 15 miles. Gordon Castle is not only much closer to the estuary but, at conditions of high tide, the water flow is reversed over a substantial part of the river. Adding to the unreliability of the Aberlour location is the discrepancy on page 430 of Strang's 1998 paper where he equates Ordnance Survey degrees latitude with Ptolemaic degrees latitude. Ptolemy gives the latitude of *Tuesis Aest.* as 59° north which Strang's table equates with OS 56°. The true OS latitude is however 57° 40′ and when the original error of Ptolemy in placing *Tuesis polis* some 10′ north of *Tuessis Aest.* is factored in, then the probability is increased that *Tuesis Polis* is located in the vicinity of Gordon Castle.

Gordon Castle, which was substantially demolished in 1953, was host, during two world wars, to the military. The grounds were probably used for military activities during the Victorian period, judging from the bits of lead and the occasional cartridge case which are found during field walking. A small part of a bronze jug was found in 1998 and preliminary examination suggested that it was of continental manufacture. Aerial photographs show a maze of crop-marks, and one, taken by Jones in 1997, is shown here *[Plate 10]*. The number of crop-marks is both daunting and encouraging.

Comyn's Road

There is a long neglected and now unused road which runs from Blair Atholl to Ruthven in Strathspey *[Figure 16]*. Known as Comyn's Road, it had fallen into disuse by the 17th century, being superseded, first by the Minigaig and then by the Wade road through Drumochter. This old road, allegedly built by an early Comyn, was intended to facilitate the transport of ale and wine from Blair Atholl to Ruthven, a distance of 43 km, compared with 67 km via Drumochter.

The Comyns are presumed to have come across from Normandy with William the Bastard; and their descendants, like so many more such as Bruce and Barclay, were invited into Scotland as agents of the 'civilising' kings of Scots. Wyntoun recounts an unlikely folk etymology that their name came from the habit of King William (1165-1214) of shouting 'come in' whenever he wanted Comyn to attend upon him.

The Comyns burst upon the historic scene during the reign of King William when John, Jordan, Richard, Walter and William appear as principals or witnesses to charters (Barrow 1971:168). In circa 1165-66 Richard is described as 'vicecommes', sheriff of Forfar while Walter and Jordan Comyn are witnesses to the same charter and are described as 'medicis' or physicians. It is obvious from the number of times that the Comyns appear in charters that by the early 13th century they were a very powerful and influential family. William married the heiress to the last Celtic earl of Buchan and by the mid 13th century, thanks to other judicious marriages, the family of Comyn held four earldoms, one lordship and thirty-two knighthoods.

One branch of this mighty family, headed by Walter, son of William, was in possession of Badenoch by circa 1230. By 1264 the Badenoch Comyn was John, grandson of William. In 1269, John annoyed the Celtic Earl of Atholl by building a castle at Blair and the dispute became so acrimonious that the king had to step in and personally settle the quarrel. It is perhaps significant that Bower (1990 Vol. 5:373), who records the incident, makes no mention of any road and considering the bad blood between Badenoch and Atholl it is most unlikely that a road would have been constructed in the years prior to 1286 when King Alexander III died and *'our golde was changit into lede'*.

However, in Macfarlane's Geographical Collections: *'Ther is a way from the yate of Blair in Atholl for carts to pass with wine, and the way is called Rad-na-pheny or way of wayne wheills, it is laid with calsay in sundrie parts.'* *Rad —na-pheny* is anglicised Gaelic for 'The Wine Road', while *calsay* means paved or cobbled. The first edition of the OS six-inch sheets named the road within Badenoch as *Rathan nan Cuimeinach*, Comyn's Road. There is little further documentary evidence of this alleged piece of medieval road building, and there is no date, prior to the Wars of Independence, circa 1296-1314, when a Comyn was in simultaneous control of both Badenoch and Atholl and thus is a position to build such a road. Unfortunately it is not clear where the march between Badenoch and Atholl was in the 13th century and, as the oldest part of Blair Castle is known as Cumming's Tower and was allegedly built by the Red (John) Comyn, then there is a possibility that the Comyns did have control of the whole route of the road. After the Wars of Independence, during which the Comyns backed the losing side, the family ceased to be of any consequence.

From the above very scanty evidence we can accept that a road, capable of carrying wheeled traffic, once existed between Blair and Ruthven, but when built or by whom is not known, but the popular belief is that it was built by a Comyn who used it to transport wine (one tradition says beer). The road fell out of use in the 16/17th centuries being superseded by the Minigaig which, in its turn, gave way to the road via Drumochter.

According to Kerr (1977:13), the road starts at Kilmaveonaig, NO880 658, a chapel on the Tilt, named after Beoghna, the abbot of Bangor who died in AD606. Despite weary and occasionally optimistic tramping over the policies of Blair Castle, there is no evidence, or rather too much evidence of tracks and trails, old and new, within the vicinity of the castle, but the 6" OS sheet of 1867 shows that the main drive into the castle might be a possible route for the road. The alleged route, on the west bank of the Banavie, becomes visible at a point near the bridge at NO859 674 and continues up the west bank of the Banavie, while across the river, on the lower flank of Meall Dubh, can be seen the abandoned settlement of Chapeltown. The track now passes the ruin of Ruichlachrie, NN819 707 then crosses the Bruar and past the cottage of Cuiltemhuc at NN816 713. The route has been lost between

Cuiltemhuc and Sron a Chleirich, but modern travellers can cross, with difficulty, Allt a Chireachain at the abandoned settlement at NN794 737 and then head for the 400m stiff climb up Sron a Chleirich where the road can be recovered as it sweeps north on the flank of the hill at NN782 769. Kerr (1977:20) writes, '*the road is even more clearly visible from the air traversing Bac na Creige and has the directness of a Roman road as it continues into Badenoch.*'

The Badenoch boundary is crossed at Back an Craig NN775 798 from where the road descends rapidly and dangerously until Allt Gharbh Ghaig is crossed by a bridge at NN777 818 and Comyn's road becomes subsumed by an ubiquitous Land Rover track to Gaick Lodge. Gaick has a black reputation in Badenoch. Anything evil or supernatural was liable to happen at Gaick. One of the Comyns (who else?) is reputed to have ordered all female workers between the ages of 12 and 30 to work naked in the fields but, when he was en route to have his lascivious way, his horse met with an accident, or perhaps the laird himself stopped an arrow, for all that was eventually found of him was a single booted leg still in the stirrup. Until Gaelic too met its death, a familiar curse in Badenoch was *Diol Bhaltair an Gaig ort*, Walter's fate in Gaick be upon you.

A more recent tragedy – though not considered as such by everybody – was the unfortunate fate of Captain John MacPherson of Ballachroan, *Othaichear Dubh*, the Black Officer. He and a few companions had gone to spend Hogmanay 1799 at Gaick, and when preparing for bed they were overwhelmed by an avalanche of such ferocity that the very barrels of their guns were twisted. A memorial stone marks where the avalanche struck, and the estate has recently erected a metal plaque with a commemorative inscription.

From Gaick there is an easily graded road along the eastern shore of Loch an t-Seolich and thence along the banks of the Tromie to Ruthven. But Comyn's road eschews the flat for the tops and any oxen dragging a wine cart would have had to cross over to the west side of the loch and then wearily wend their way up on to the shoulder of Boghacloiche, NN745 865, and then straight ahead via Maol an t-Seolich and Drum an t-Seilich before dropping down to Bhran at NN753 913. From Bhran, ahead stretches Glen Tromie with a very gentle gradient down the Spey, but once again Comyn's road heads for the heights, past Carn Pheigith, NN755 934 and Sron na Gaoithe where it joins a slightly more distinct path at NN759 958 and then it is downhill all the way round the west flank of Beinn Bhuidhe to meet the B970 road at NN764 996, just opposite Ruthven barracks.

The ostensible reason for building such an expensive and difficult road was to transport wine. But would it be necessary to build a road for such a purpose, which could have been solved by hanging a couple of barrels over a garron and sending it on with a ghillie? An ox wagon required a whole team of leaders, whippers, goaders etc. Such an apparition heading for the high tops must have been easily visible and probably required an armed escort to ensure its safe arrival. Gaick was well within the jurisdiction of Badenoch, so once having reached there the wine would have been safe from the most desperate of villains; yet, from Gaick, the road does not take the easy option but heads for the high tops, and later, at Bhran, takes the same more difficult option. When faced with the possibility of an easier route the road builders chose the high ground with enhanced visibility. The road may have taken wheeled traffic but it was not well designed to do so. It was built to connect two places by the shortest possible route and was built as high as possible to minimise the possibility of ambush.

This type of road-building was favoured by the Romans, many examples of which can still be clearly seen from the air in the Near and Middle East (Baradez 1949, Kennedy and Riley 1990) and are described, alas with few illustrations, by Margary (1973). If Comyn's road was built by the Romans, it must have been to link two places of strategic importance. Only some 40km south of Blair are the foundations of their great legionary fortress of Inchtuthil. It would have been remiss of

the Romans to have built such a strategic stronghold without the means
to rapidly transport their troops to any trouble spot. Beyond the bulk of
the Cairngorms lay Moray, with its garrisons and naval base, and a road
there by the most direct route and immune to ambush was the obvious
requirement.

At Ruthven in Strathspey there are the ruins of Wade's barracks,
built on the foundations of the earlier Comyn castle, which in its turn
was probably placed on the site of a prehistoric fortress. But the mound
is unlikely to have had anything to do with the Romans who preferred a
wide range of fire and the possibilities of disciplined manoeuvres by
troops who were trained to move in formation. Such sites are sometimes
found on the floodplain of a river and it so happens that an old estate
map, RHP 1859, shows such a site. This also corresponds with the
tradition that there was a Roman camp between Ruthven and Pitmain.
A camp, which despite intensive aerial photography during summer and
winter, has not yet been revealed.

There is insufficient evidence to claim that Comyn's road was built
by the Romans, but neither is there evidence that it was built by the
Comyns. It merits much closer unbiased scrutiny. The level ground at
Giack and Bhran should be examined for evidence of Roman-style earth
works, while the road profile and construction could well be examined
where they still survive. Tacitus states that Agricola marched back to
base from the battle of Mons Graupius by a different route to that used
in his advance. Not far from Ruthven is the great hilltop fortress of Dun
da Lamh, controlling the whole of upper Strathspey, and well within its
curtilage are the low sharp peaks of Crùban Mór and Cruban Beag.
Perhaps the site of the battle of Mons Graupius? And from where
Agricola marched his troops south over a route which, subsequently
tidied up by the legions in the next two years, was eventually to be
credited to the activities of a powerful family with the name of Comyn.

References

Baradez, J. *Fossatum Africa*, Paris. 1949

Barr, D. *The Spey from Source to Sea*, Moray Society Lecture, Elgin. 2004

Barrow, G. W. S. *Acts of Malcolm IV*, Edinburgh. 1971

Bower, W., ed. Watt, D. E. R. *Scotichronicon* Vol. 5, Aberdeen. 1990

Douglas, R. *Annals of the Royal Burgh of Forres*, Elgin. 1934

Forbes, F. 'Parish of Grange' in *OSA*, Edinburgh. 1791

Forbes, L. W. 'Parish of Boharm' in *NSA*, Edinburgh. 1834

Hunter, F. 'Roman and Native in Scotland: new approaches' in *Journal of Roman Archaeology* Vol. 14. 2001

Jackson, K. H. in *The Problem of the Picts*, ed. Wainwright, F. T., Edinburgh. 1955

Kennedy, D. & Riley, D. *Rome's Desert Frontier from the Air*, London. 1990

Keui, J. *Old Grampian Highways*, Inverness. 1977

Leslie, F. 'Parish of Boharm' in *OSA*, Edinburgh. 1795

Margary, I. D. *Roman Roads in Britain*, 3rd edition, London. 1973

Müller, C. *Ptolemaei Geographiae* Lib. II, Cap. 3., Paris, 1883-1901

REM = Cockburn, H. T. ed. *Registrum Episcoptus Moraviensis (Moray Register)*, Edinburgh. 1837

Rivet, A. L. F. & Smith, C. *The Place-Names of Roman Britain*, London. 1979

Stevenson, E. L. ed. *Claudius Ptolemy - The Geography*, London. 1932, 1991

Strang, A. 'Explaining Ptolemy's Roman Britain' in *Britannia* Vol. xxviii. 1997

Strang, A. 'Recreating a possible Flavian map of Roman Britain with a detailed map for Scotland' in *PSAS* Vol. 128. 1998

St. Joseph, J. K. 'Air Reconnaissance of North Britain' in *JRS* Vol. xli. 1951

Watson, W. J. *History of the Celtic Place-Names of Scotland*, Edinburgh. 1926

Plate 1: Tarradale

Plate 2: Balnageith

Plate 3: Balnageith: Revetted Sump

Plate 4: Easter Galcantry

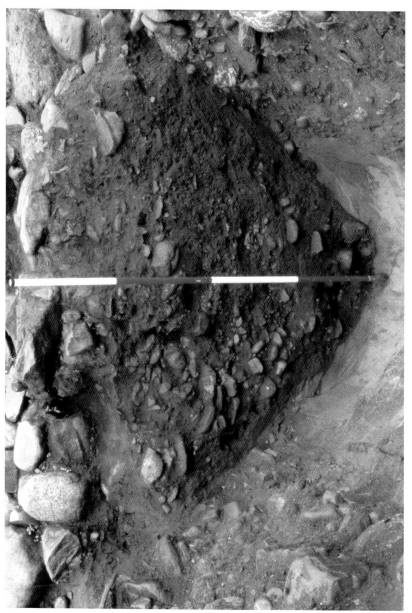

Plate 5: Easter Galcantry: Recu± Ditch

Plate 6: Birnie: The First Hoard (Kenny Williamson)

Plate 7: Birnie: The First Hoard (Kenny Williamson)

Plate 8: Birnie: The Second Hoard
(Trustees of the National Museums of Scotland)

Plate 9: Birnie Kirk

Plate 10: Gordon Castle Precincts

Abbreviations

JRS	Journal of the Roman Society
NSA	New Statistical Account
OD	Ordnance Datum - above sea level
OS	Ordnance Survey
OSA	Old Statistical Account
P-Celtic	Ancestral Welsh
Proc.Soc.Ant.Scot./PSAS	Proceedings of the Society of Antiquaries of Scotland
Q-Celtic	Ancestral to Irish and Scottish Gaelic
REM	*Registrum Episcoptus Moraviensis (Moray Register)*
SAS	Society of Antiquaries of Scotland
SJ	Society of Jesus
SRS	Society for Roman Studies
Trans.North.AssLit& Scien.Soc.	Transactions of the Northern Association of Literary and Scientific Societies

Bibliography

Anderson, J. G. C. *Cornelii Taciti - De Vita Agricolae*, Oxford. 1953

Archaeologia Vol. lxiv, London. 1912/3

Arrand, D. *Britain under and after the Romans*, Birmingham. 1997

Aubrey, J. *Monumenta Britannica* Vols I and II, Sherbourne. 1982

Baradez, J. *Fossatum Africa*, Paris. 1949

Barrett, J. C. et al *Barbarians and Romans in North-West Europe*, Oxford. 1989

Baume, P. la *The Romans on the Rhine*, Bonn. 1975

Bédoyère, G. de la *The Finds of Roman Britain*, London. 1989

Berger, H. *Geschichte der wissenschaftlichen Erdkunde der Griechen*, Leipzig. 1903

Blaeu, J. *Atlas Novus*, Amsterdam. 1654

Breeze, D. J. *The Northern Frontiers of Roman Britain*, London. 1982

Breeze, D. J. *The Second Augustan Legion in North Britain*, Cardiff. 1989

Burn, A. R. *Agricola and Roman Britain*, London. 1965

Caesar, J. *The Conquest of Gaul*, Penguin. 1972

Chalmers, G. *Caledonia*, Edinburgh. 1807, 1810, 1824

Connolly, P. *Greece and Rome at War*, London. 1988

Cottrell, L. *The Great Invasion*, London. 1958

Crawford, O. G. S. *Topography of Roman Scotland*, Cambridge. 1949

Cunliffe, B. W. ed. *Excavations of the Roman Fort at Richborough*, Oxford. 1968

Davies, G. et al. eds. *Trac 2000*, Oxford. 2001

Dilke, O. A. W. *Greek and Roman Maps*, London. 1985

Dorey, T. A. ed. *Tacitus*, London. 1969

Douglas, R. *Annals of the Royal Burgh of Forres*, Elgin. 1934

Ellegård, C. & Åkerström-Hougen, G. eds. *Rome and the North*, Sweden. 1996

Freeman, P. et al. eds. *Limes* Vol. xviii, *Jordan 2000*, Oxford. 2002

Frere, S. *Britannia - A History of Roman Britain*, London. 1987

Frere, S. S. & St. Joseph, J. K. *Roman Britain from the Air*, Cambridge. 1983

Gilliver, C. M. *The Roman Art of War*, Stroud. 2001

Gordon, R. *Blaeu's Atlas*, Amsterdam. 1654

Grant, E. *Memoirs of a Highland Lady*, London. 1950

Groenman-van Waateringe, W. et al. eds. *Roman Frontier Studies*, Oxford. 1997

Handford, S. A. trans. *Caesar - The Conquest of Gaul*, Penguin. 1951

Hanson, W. & Maxwell, G. *Rome's North West Frontier*, Edinburgh. 1983

Hanson, W. *Agricola and the Conquest of the North*, London. 1991

Henderson, A. R. 'From 83 to 1983: *On the Trail of Mons Graupius'* in *The Deeside Field* 18, Aberdeen. 1984

Horsley, J. *Britannia Romana*, London, 1733 & Newcastle, 1974

Hyland, A. *Training the Roman Cavalry*, Stroud. 1993

Jameson, J. *Remarks on the Progress of the Roman Army in Scotland*, London. 1786

Jones, G. D. B. *Concept and Development in Roman Frontiers*, Manchester. 1978

Jones, G. D. B. & Mattingly, D. *An Atlas of Roman Britain*, Oxford. 1990

Jones, G. D. B. & Wooliscroft, D. J. *Hadrian's Wall from the Air*, Stroud. 2001

Kamm, A. *The Last Frontier - The Roman Invasions of Scotland*, Stroud. 2004

Kennedy, D. ed. *Into the Sun*, Sheffield. 1989

Kennedy, D. & Riley, D. *Rome's Desert Frontier from the Air*, London. 1990

Keppie, L. *Scotland's Roman Remains*, Edinburgh. 1986

Kerr, J. *Old Grampian Highways*, Inverness. 1977

Le Bohec, Y. *The Imperial Roman Army*, London. 1994

Lindsay, A. *A Rutter of the Scottish Seas*, Maritime Monograph No. 44, Greenwich. 1980

Luttwak, E. *The Grand Strategy of the Roman Empire*, Baltimore. 1976

MacDonald, G. *The Roman Wall in Scotland*, Edinburgh. 1934

Marren, P. *Grampian Battlefields*, Aberdeen. 1990

Marsden, E. W. *Greek & Roman Artillery*, Oxford. 1999

Mason, D. J. P. *Roman Britain and the Roman Navy*, Stroud. 2003

Mattingly, D. J. et al. *Studi Miscellanei Romano-Libyan Settlement*, Rome. 1990

Mattingly, H. trans. *Tacitus - The Agricola and the Germania*, Penguin. 1970

Maxfield, V. A. & Dobson, M. J. *Roman Frontier Studies 1989*, Exeter. 1991

Maxwell, G. *The Romans in Scotland*, Edinburgh. 1989

Maxwell, G. *A Battle Lost: Romans and Caledonians at Mons Graupius*, Edinburgh. 1990

Moore, R. W. ed. *The Romans in Britain*, London. 1968

Morrison, J. S. & Coates, J. F. *The Athenian Tireme: The history and reconstruction of an ancient Greek warship*, Cambridge. 1986

Müller, C. *Ptolemaei Geographiae*, Paris. 1883-1901

Nicolaisen, W. F. H. *Scottish Place-Names*, London. 1976

Muir, R. *History from the Air*, London. 1983

Ogilvie, R. M. & Richmond, I. *De Vita Agricolae*, Oxford. 1967

Peddie, J. *Conquest - The Roman Invasion of Britain*, Stroud. 1998

Pitts, L. F. & St. Joseph, J. K. *Inchtuthil, the Roman legionary fortress*, London. 1975

Ptolemaei, C. *Cosmographia*, Leicester. 1990

REM = Cockburn, H. T. ed. *Registrum Episcoptus Moraviensis (Moray Register)*, Edinburgh. 1837

Richmond, I. A. *Roman and Native in North Britain*, Edinburgh. 1961

Riley, D. N. *Air Photography & Archaeology*, Philadelphia. 1987

Rivet, A. L. F. & Smith, C. *The Place-Names of Roman Britain*, London. 1979

Roy, W. 'The Military Antiquities of the Romans' in *North Britain*, London. 1793

SAS, *PSAS* Vols. lxviii, lxvviv, xciv, ciii, cxxviii, cxxxi, Edinburgh. 1916-2001

Sellar, W. D. H. *Moray Province and People*, Edinburgh. 1993

Smith, R. *Grampian Ways*, Melven Press, Perth. 1980

Smout, T. C. ed. *Scotland and the Sea*, Edinburgh. 1992

Spaul, J. *Classes Imperii Romani*, Nectoreca, Andover. 2002

SRS, *Britannia* Vol. i - Vol. xxxv, London. 1969-2004

SRS, *JRS* Vols. xli, li, lv, lxi, lxvii, London. 1951, 1961, 1965, 1971, 1977

Starr, C. G. *Roman Imperial Navy 31BC - AD324 3rd edition*, Ares Publishers. 1993

Stevenson, E. L. ed. *Claudius Ptolemy - The Geography*, London. 1932, 1991

Stuart, R. *Caledonia Romana*, Edinburgh. 1845

Thomson, O. *The Romans in Scotland*, London. 1969

Todd, M. ed. *Research on Roman Britain 1960-89*, London. 1989

Wainright, F. T. ed. *The Problem of the Picts*, Edinburgh. 1955

Watts, D. *Christian and Pagans in Roman Britain*, London. 1991

Watson, W. J. *History of the Celtic Place-Names of Scotland*, Edinburgh. 1926

Webster, G. *The Roman Army*, Chester. 1956

Webster, G. *The Roman Imperial Army*, London. 1969

Webster, G. & Dudley, D. R. *The Roman Conquest of Britain*, London. 1965

Williamson, G. A. *Josephus - The Jewish War*, Penguin. 1959

Wilson, D. R. *Roman Frontiers of Britain*, London. 1968

Wilson, D. R. *Air Photo Interpretation for Archaeologists*, Stroud, 2000

Wooliscroft, D. J. *The Roman Frontier on the Gask Ridge, Perth and Kinross*, Oxford. 2002

Young, R. *Notes on Burghead: Ancient and Modern*, Elgin. 1868